# ANTHROPOLOGICAL LINGUISTICS

*An Introduction*

STUDIES IN
ANTHROPOLOGY

*Consulting Editors:*

MORTON H. FRIED
AND MARVIN HARRIS
*Columbia University*

# ANTHROPOLOGICAL
# LINGUISTICS

---

## *An Introduction*

BY JOSEPH H. GREENBERG

*Stanford University*

R A N D O M   H O U S E   ·   N E W   Y O R K

P121
G74

# Preface

When I was first invited by Marvin Harris and Morton Fried to write a book on language for the Random House Studies in Anthropology series, they stated that at least for some of the projected works they were "looking forward as much to creative synthesis as traditional coverage." They wondered, however, whether this applied as much to language as to other topics, since they were "led to believe that linguistics already has a firm taxonomic and methodological foundation." At the time that they wrote this, much that had been generally accepted as part of this foundation was already being shaken by the first substantial impact of transformation theory on American and world linguistics. It was necessary, therefore, for me to attempt the second alternative: a restatement of what seems to have survived as the fundamental viewpoint and achievement in linguistics. In this task I have been guided by the belief that the most fundamental goal of linguistics, as of any other empirical science, is the attainment of lawlike generalizations.

Given the basically nonspecialist audience to which the books in this series are directed and the limitations in length, I have tried to treat in an introductory and essentially nontechnical fashion some of the topics that form the core of linguistics as a science. If the present work succeeds in this aim, it should help undergraduate and graduate students at the earlier stages of their training, particularly in disciplines other than linguistics, to gain a preliminary notion of the basic nature and goals of that discipline.

I wish particularly to express my appreciation to Marvin Harris and Morton Fried, the general editors of the series, for their assistance in preparing this book; to Dorothy Kaschube, who read the work in manuscript; and to my faithful typist, Mrs. Katie Weers.

*Stanford, California*                                                   J. H. G.
*May, 1968*

# Contents

# ANTHROPOLOGICAL LINGUISTICS

*An Introduction*

# THE NATURE AND DEFINITION
# OF LANGUAGE

Of the myriad species that inhabit the earth, man is unique in the complexity of his institutions and the extent of his mastery of the inanimate and animate environments. Anthropologists and other social scientists agree that this is due to a uniquely human mode of adaptation, the cultural. Man has grown taller than the giraffe and tunneled more deeply in the earth than the mole, not by evolving a longer neck or a more efficient snout, either of which would probably take him many thousands of years, but through an accumulation of knowledge and skills. Moreover, each new human being does not have to face his environment on the basis of his individual equipment and experience. He grows up in the midst of one or another of a large number of human groups, through which he acquires knowledge, technological skills, modes of interpersonal adjustment, values, beliefs, and much else with which he confronts the world. This accumulation constitutes the non-biological inheritance that we call the culture of the particular group.

Among all the aspects of the cultural inheritance, anthropologists are virtually unanimous in pointing to two, tools and speech, as the most fundamental, in that they provide the indispensable prerequisites for the remainder.

With regard to tools, a certain clarification is necessary. We are talking here of toolmaking, not tool use. Man's closest biological relative, the anthropoid ape, in this respect as in others, closely foreshadows human development. Anthropoid apes as well as certain other primates, notably baboons, use as tools objects that are already found in the environment, such as sticks or stones. Only man makes tools, however, in the sense that he modifies objects that he finds so as to produce new artificial objects that are adapted to some specific end. A seemingly marginal case is Köhler's chimpanzee Sultan, who in a famous experiment fitted together two sticks with which he then knocked down a banana that he could not otherwise reach. While Sultan did produce an object that he did not find in his environment, the sticks had previously been fashioned by human carpenters to fit together. Without the prodding of the human experimenter, even Sultan would not have selected two sticks of his own accord and then put them together to form the tool he needed. At least, no nonhuman species has ever been observed to behave in this or in any comparable fashion on its own.

The two basic human traits of toolmaking and speech are more similar to each other than might appear at first glance. They have in common indirectness of action on the environment—the natural environment, for tools; the social environment, in the case of speech. By means of tools, man extends the sphere of his action through manipulation of some physical object that is not part of his own body. In some of the simplest instances, the tool functions as an artificial limb. A stick, for example, is an artificial hand, that will move an object that is not within reach of the hand itself. Similarly, through speech, man can bring a fellow human being to do something for him—for example, to throw down an apple from a tree, when it is beyond his own reach. It is indeed as a tool of social interaction and cooperation that speech most clearly confers an evolutionary advantage on man.

Toolmaking and speech are interrelated in yet another way. One may conceive of the utilization of very simple tools, such as sticks, as taking place in the absence of speech. This is indeed the case with tool-using primates. By contrast, at the simplest level of human tool behavior, a stick or a rock is modified in form so as to make it more useful for some intended purpose. In such instances, some symbolic substitute is plainly necessary for the object that is not yet present. The inventiveness that is required for the production of such relatively elementary devices as the fire drill is evidently far beyond the capacities of even the most intelligent nonhumans. It demands the capacity to solve mechanical problems imaginatively, by way of constructions that will produce objects not encountered in nature. Such efforts of constructive imagination do not seem possible without the instrument of language.

When we find, in the archeological record, specific types of such purposefully fashioned tools persisting over time in the form of a definite toolmaking tradition, we see a cultural trait that, we assume, could not have come into existence without language. From its transmission we infer the operation of a fundamental function of language: the communication of already acquired knowledge. This indirect evidence makes it highly probable that the earlier nonsapiens human species, which can be shown by archeological evidence to have fashioned tools and transmitted the appropriate techniques from generation to generation, likewise had language. If the inference from this evidence is valid, then language is several million years old.

Although two or three million years seems like a very long time, it is only a brief moment in the tremendous perspective of geological time, within which life has existed for several billions of years. Language is therefore a recent phenomenon, coincident with and intimately related to the emergence of humanity itself within the evolutionary process.

The radically new type of adjustment that language makes possible clearly qualifies it as an evolutionary emergent of fundamental significance, in that it initiated a distinctly new stage of development, comparable to the genesis of life itself and to the first appearance of intelligence. Investigation of the way in which the emergence of language took place has so far produced a vast speculative literature, but not yet an answer that is generally agreed on and satisfactory. Part of the perennial fascination of the problem lies in the belief that, since all the evidence points to the existence of an extremely long prelinguistic period and, since the fact that language now exists means that it must have arisen at some point in time, the problem of how it arose does have an answer. Since direct verification is impossible, however, we can never be sure that we have the correct solution. It is also somewhat strange and disconcerting that what must have been a creature without language somehow developed into one with language, while we who have language ourselves do not know how it happened.

It is not my purpose to add still another to the theories that already exist in this field. It seems safe to assume, however, that language did not spring from nothing. It must have been preceded by and genetically developed out of something else that, while it lacked the essential qualities of language, shared with it some common formal and functional ground. The most obvious candidate for this role is communication by vocal gesture, such as is found among the anthropoid apes; in type at least, this probably represents one of the earlier stages out of which language grew. There may well have been other intermediate forms, which are not found among apes and yet are not language. In short, language is one species of a genus, the genus of communication.

From this relationship three basic and interrelated questions arise. One, which has already been broached and is, in fact, the traditional way of approaching the problem, is the question of origin: In what way did language arise out of nonlanguage during the course of historical development? The second question is definitional: What distinguishes human language as a communication system from other forms of communication? The third is psychological: What capacities are required for language behavior? Do they involve a mere increase in complexity of basically the same psychological abilities as are found in nonhuman species? Or do all other animals lack the biological endowment that is necessary for the acquisition of language, so that it is in principle impossible for them to acquire it? Some psychologists apparently believe that the more highly endowed species are in principle capable of acquiring language and have therefore tried to develop language in chimpanzees, thus far without success.

Of the three approaches indicated above—the historical, the definitional, and the psychological—we shall be concerned chiefly with the second. In a way, it is prior to the other two, for until we have determined what is essential in human language, as distinct from other means of communication, we shall lack a criterion of success for the other two enterprises. It is not rare for theories of origin or psychological theories concerning language to be advanced in which the implicit notion of what constitutes a language is defective, in that some essential characteristic is not taken into consideration.

My own point of departure has been the view that language is only one of a number of actual or potential types of communication. Language will therefore both resemble and differ from other modes of communication. The similarity of language to certain other phenomena is prefigured in the tendency to use the word "language" in various extended senses. Thus, forms of animal communication are sometimes called "languages" in the literature on the subject. Mathematics has been regarded as a language, as in the eloquent statement by Galileo in which secrets of the universe are likened to a book that we cannot understand until we know the language in which it is written, and this language is mathematics.[1] Music is sometimes called "the universal language." With such usage I have no quarrel. My concern here is with the definition of human language in the restricted sense, and it is in that way that I use the word "language." The alternative would be to use some such term as "human language" to designate the object of my enquiry.

We have a particularly detailed account of gibbon communication by Carpenter, who lists "nine types of the more prominent and more easily differentiated sound patterns produced by the gibbon." [2] He notes that "their functions are extremely difficult to infer" but adds that "the fact is clear that these vocalizations as well as other sound patterns not only express excitement in an individual but also they have communicative, signaling value or instrumental value."

Carpenter describes each of these nine types in terms of stimulus situation, subjects (i.e., emitters of the signal in question), animal responding, responses, and probable function. The following examples may serve as illustrations. The second of Carpenter's nine types is a cry that is given either early in the morning or when the group is in motion. It is emitted by adult males and takes the form of single discrete calls, "a series but may be repeated over and over again"; it is responded to by animals in neighboring groups, which make similar calls either simultaneously or alternately. Its probable function is described as that of localizing the group in its territory and thus avoiding intergroup conflict. The ninth type is emitted by the group leader during group progression and consists of a "chatter or series of clicks." The response of the group is to follow the leader, in this case without vocalization. Its probable function is described as that of "directing group progression."

If we view this as a system of communication, we find a number of significant differences from human linguistic communication. Of these, three are most germane to the present discussion: the nature of the "meanings" being signaled; the absence of grammatical structure; and the absence of an articulate phonetic level, as distinct from a semantic level. The nature of the meaning is suggested by the fact that Carpenter does not try to give a "translation" of the message. What might correspond to meaning he describes under "probable function," such as group localization and avoidance of conflict, as indicated in the first examples cited. The indefiniteness of the message can be seen if we do attempt to translate it. We may view it either as referential, announcing something like "This is our territory," or imperative "Keep away!" Indeed we can interpret this vocalization as merely a kind of spontaneous noisemaking, linked with rising in the morning or with a group movement that is taken to be a sign of the presence of the first group in a particular location. We are still closer to expressive behavior that is capable of being interpreted as a sign by another organism than we are to well-codified purposive communication. Even if we take it to be the latter, we may nevertheless say that it does not differentiate such modes as the indicative or the referential from the imperative. It is not so much that human language is referential while gibbon communication is not, but that human language differentiates modes, among which the referential is one, whereas in anthropoid communication there is no evidence that these are distinguished.

A second basic difference is that each gibbon cry is a separate and discrete signal, which does not combine with others to form messages that are more complex and analyzable. In human speech the unit of functional communication is the sentence, which is analyzable into parts—roughly speaking, words; these may enter into varied combinations and most of them—that is, those parts of sentences that have independent content as against those with grammatical function—point to some aspect of the particular situation. The rules regarding possible combinations of those components may be called grammatical structure. The existence of a complex grammatical structure, in which independently meaningful elements may combine in various ways, and in which some elements may have functions remote from the simple referring to a class of present objects, qualities or activities, opens up vast possibilities that are not found in any animal communication. Man entertains hypotheses, asks questions, lies, discourses about the past, and discusses future plans: this is indeed what makes him the "time-binding animal." The gibbon can only signal about the here and now.

The third difference may appear to be more superficial —a mere technical device, as it were. But it is a technical device of vast efficacy, without which human language as we know it would hardly be possible. This difference is the articulate basis of speech, in the form of a limited number of distinct sound units, commonly called phonemes. These number from about 10 to 70 in individual languages; each of them by itself has no meaning, yet in particular sequences they form meaningful units. When speech is represented by alphabetic writing, then the individual letters or combinations of letters correspond roughly to the phonemes, and the thousands of separate words are meaningful combinations formed out of these elementary units. It is clear that the anthropoid method of individually different sounds for each meaning would soon reach a dead end, in that the number of consistently, distinguishably different calls must be rather small. On the other hand, only 10 phonemic units, themselves meaningless, will provide 10,000 different sequences of length 4 (i.e., $10^4$). No other available method seems to be capable of forming the thousands of distinguishably different meaningful units of human speech.

This characteristic of human speech has been described

as a duality, since it involves two levels of functioning: the sound level, in which the units are inherently meaningless phonemes, and the meaningful level, in which the units are words or other units that are involved in grammatical constructions. Every theory of linguistic description must deal in some fashion with this distinction between phonological and grammatical level.

Of these three differences—multimodality, grammaticity, and duality—it is the second, the existence of analyzable grammatical structure in every human message, that has seemed in the past to linguists to be the most essential characteristic of human language, a sufficient basis for distinguishing human language from all forms of communication by subhuman species.

Nevertheless, the diffusion among linguists of the basic facts about the remarkable system of bee communication that has been described in the pioneering work of Von Frisch has raised serious doubts about the adequacy of grammaticity as the distinguishing criterion for human communication.[3] After a scouting bee has found a source of honey, on returning to the hive he begins a figure-eight dance. The speed of the dance—that is, the number of figures completed in a unit time—is related to the distance of the source; the livelier the dance, the nearer the source of honey. The direction is indicated by the angle of the dance to the surface of the hive; this corresponds to the angle of the source of honey to the sun. With the information communicated by this dance, bees who have not seen the source of honey are able to go out on their own and find it.

Bee communication evidently involves a complex signaling whole which, like the sentence in human language, is analyzable into a combination of meaningful units. In this case there are two such units, one indicating the distance, the other the direction of the source. It would seem then that grammaticity is not the exclusive property of humans and cannot be the defining characteristic of human language. Further, the most natural "translation" of a bee message seems to be referential: "There is a source of honey at a certain distance and in a certain direction." We could also perhaps interpret the message as "Come and get it!"; if we maintain the referential translation, however, then another supposedly human attribute must be shared with the bees. However, we have here pointed to the formal distinction of modes in human language rather than to the existence of any particular one—the declarative or the referential, for example—as essential. In this sense, human language is multimodal and bee communication unimodal.

In still another way, the discoveries about bee communication have exerted a profoundly disturbing and at the same time stimulating effect on the thinking of linguists. It had often been noted by linguists that human language has a characteristic that they have called "productivity"— namely, that it is possible to interpret a message that has never occurred before. In fact, we are constantly forming and interpreting sentences that have probably never been encountered in our experience. Clearly, gibbon signaling is not productive in this sense, but bee communication is: a bee can find a source of honey by means of a message type he has never received before. Incidentally, this property of both human and bee communication rules out any very simple psychological theory of meaning, such as is based on the association in past experience between a particular message and its meaning.

Of the three characteristics described earlier, therefore, only duality would seem to hold up unambiguously as distinguishing human from bee communication. On closer scrutiny, however, it appears that we need not confine ourselves to duality and that an essential difference does appear on the grammatical level. For the bee message always contains two and only two meaningful components. Now it is not only true of human sentences that they may contain more than two meaningful units—for example, words—but that there is no limit in principle to the length of these sentences. We cannot say of a particular English sentence, however long it is, that it is the longest possible sentence; there are built into the grammar of English, and indeed of every natural language, devices by which it is always possible to build longer sentences than any given sentence—for example, by adding *and the moon is made of green cheese,* or by attaching an additional adjectival modifier to any noun.

There seems then to be a real difference in principle between bee communication, with its two meaningful units, and human language, with its unlimited complexity of sentences. If there were a longest sentence in English, then all the sentences in the language could be listed in order of length and so numbered. Since this cannot be done, the number of sentences is infinite. By definition, for example, the set of natural numbers is infinite: if we are given any finite set as the set of all numbers, we can always add a new one by way of the next higher number to the largest in the given set. Now all natural numbers can be expressed in English, and yet this is but a minor subset of English expressions.[4]

It might be argued that in bee communication there is also an infinity of possible messages, since there is a continuum of distance and a continuum of direction. This would be a different kind of infinity, however, that of infinitesimal differences. In practice, this argument breaks down since there are differences in the speed of the dance and in its direction that are too small to be taken into account. The absence of any limit to the number of meaningful elements in a message in human language therefore remains a basic point of distinction between it and the language of bees.

If we accept as reasonable the argument above, that bee communication does in fact have a finitude of messages, then we can see that productivity and infinity are not identical. While bee communication is productive, it is not infinite. Indeed, if a finite system has some higher-level principle of organization, it then becomes possible to understand a message that has not been received before. In the case of the bees, it is the regular mapping of distance and direction into another set of dimensions, speed and angle of dance— a mapping in which the relations of greater and smaller, more and less, are invariant—that makes productivity possible. Technically, such types of mapping are called *icons*. Another important difference between human language and bee communication now appears, in that there is no such regular relation between sign and meaning in human speech. The relation is rather one of arbitrariness, in the sense of the nonpredictability of meaning from sound. In such cases, it is customary to speak of symbols. Thus, language is symbolic, whereas bee communication is iconic.

We have not yet, however, touched upon what appears to be the most fundamental difference, one that, as will be shown, implies all the rest and moreover helps to distinguish language from still other methods of communication than that of bees or anthropoid apes. This characteristic we shall call "semantic universality." When we consider the semantic content of bee communication, what strikes us is its narrowness. It is concerned only with sources of honey, which is no doubt an eternally fascinating subject to bees, but still a very restricted one. In human language, we can talk about anything that bees talk about, as well as innumerable other subjects. Whenever everything that can be said in one system of communication A can be translated into another system B, while not everything that can be said in B can be translated into A, we say that B is semantically more comprehensive than A. In this sense, any human language is more comprehensive than either bee or gibbon communication.

It is also possible to assert that any natural language is semantically more comprehensive than any other system of communication. This characteristic of all natural languages is what is referred to above as semantic universality,[5] which also seems to entail the other characteristics we have thus far found to hold for all natural languages, in contrast with the systems of animal communication we have considered. The ability to deal with such a wide range of subject matter calls for a large stock of meaningful elements; hence the need for duality, and for an infinite grammatical structure. Further, iconicity, as opposed to the arbitrariness of human symbolic communication, breaks down when it is applied to a complex or abstract subject matter, just as picture-writing is by itself inadequate to represent the structure of spoken language.

A final comparison that will prove instructive is that with another human symbolic system, mathematics. Mathematics resembles a language in that it has statements that are analyzable into individual meaningful symbols, which have combined to produce these and other messages. Moreover, infinity of messages is found in mathematics, as it is in natural languages. Indeed, this is implied in our earlier argument that the infinity of natural languages could be proved by the infinity of natural numbers expressible in it. Yet these are but one part of mathematical expressions, too, so that mathematics has not only grammaticity but infinite grammaticity. Thus mathematics has a number of those important characteristics of language that are lacking in bee communication. Yet the key characteristic of semantic universality is lacking.

It is true that every mathematical statement can be made in ordinary language. In fact, we define more complex mathematical concepts in terms of basic concepts that have been derived from everyday life and ordinary language— for example, numbers and addition. But the opposite does not hold: there is no mathematical translation of *Pass me the water* or *Where are my glasses?* or of an infinite number of other sentences of ordinary language. Two other characteristics of language that seem to survive the test of comparison with mathematics are multimodality and duality: mathematics seems to have only the single mode of assertion; further, mathematical symbols are meaningful in themselves, and are not resolvable into more elementary units without meaning, such as would correspond to the phonemes of spoken language or the letters of written language.

Of the three characteristics that have thus far remained as unique to language—multimodality, duality, and semantic universality—the first, while exclusive to human communication systems in general, seems on reflection not necessarily to be confined to language. Formal, logical symbolisms have been devised that, like mathematics, may be considered to be symbol systems and that incorporate various modes besides the indicative—for example, possibility. These symbol systems are able to express propositions of the type "A may be true."

Thus far, the term *language* has been used without distinction between its spoken and written forms. The former has usually been intended, since it is primary in a number of ways (to be discussed later), of which the most obvious is that it arose earlier in evolution; every individual, moreover, learns to speak before he writes, and, indeed, many individuals who speak a language never learn to write it. In some discussions of the subject, only spoken language is meant by the term *language*, and the use of sound as a medium is therefore included in the definition. It has seemed more useful in the present context to consider language in terms of its structural characteristics, rather than in terms of the physical medium employed. On this basis, both spoken and written languages (and any further representations, such as Morse code, which is based on spoken or written language) are to be regarded as language. This is in accordance with common usage. In principle, moreover, with a few limitations, for any language that exists in both forms there is a one-to-one mapping on the sentence level. Every spoken sentence has an orthographic representation, and every written sentence can be read.[6]

There are two main systems of writing. In the phonetic system, the individual symbols correspond, with varying degrees of complexity, to individual phonemes, or in some systems to syllables. The other system may be called ideographic, in that each written symbol represents a meaning-ful unit, usually a word. Phonetic systems of writing reflect the structure of all spoken languages, in respect to duality, in that there is both a phonetic and a grammatical level. Ideographic systems, such as the Chinese, however, do not have duality, since there is no phonological level as such. Hence, we are finally left with semantic universality as a sufficient condition for the defining of language, in the sense in which it is employed here.

# II

_____

# LINGUISTICS AS A SCIENCE

Every academic discipline involves the use of linguistic data. The historian, for example, works chiefly with written documents, whose linguistic interpretation is a prerequisite for their use as sources of historical inference. The field ethnologist, in observing the behavior of an alien culture, uses the results of recorded interviews and also, if he has sufficient command of the language, what he has heard in other, noninterview situations. The legal scholar concerns himself with the problems of the interpretation of statutes; sometimes he seeks to determine the intent of the lawmakers from the records of their debates. The physicist must on occasion examine critically the terminology of his own science; in general, moreover, he is expected to describe his apparatus, record his observations, and state his theory in linguistic form, even though some of his data may also contain a mathematical component. The literary scholar's object of study is, of course, wholly linguistic.

Reflection on these and similar examples suggests that language enters into the various sciences and disciplines in two ways—as subject matter and as the instrument for the making of descriptive or theoretical statements. In the first respect, its role may vary from constituting the entire subject matter (literature), part of the subject matter (ethnology), or none of it (physics). In the latter respect, however, all fields of inquiry are more or less involved: all will on occasion not only use language for theoretical purposes, but also talk about its theoretical use, in metatheoretical discussion. There is indeed one subject matter that, in the opinion of some, consists of nothing but this—namely, the philosophy of science, which is concerned with the analysis of the language of science.

For all these linguistic concerns of the various sciences, there is one science, linguistics, which takes its name from language and is therefore, one might suspect, occupied with language in some fashion that is fundamentally different from the concern with language on the part of the other sciences. Every other science, insofar as it is concerned with linguistic data, concerns itself with them as a means to an end. Only linguistics is interested in language as an end in itself. All other disciplines, including even literature, which has a purely linguistic subject matter, are interested in the specific content or meaning of a particular set of language data. In terms of information theory, all the other sciences are interested in certain messages from the standpoint of their contents—for example, legal texts, poems, informant statements (ethnology), patient protocols (clinical psychology). Only linguistics is interested in the code per se in accordance with whose rules the messages are sent. Other sciences learn these codes in order to interpret messages sent in them. Linguistics uses messages as evidence of the structure of the code in which they are sent, the messages themselves being of no intrinsic interest, except as exemplifications of rules of the code. In fact, there is a long-standing practice in accordance with which a fair proportion of the sentences used for illustrative purposes in grammars are inherently silly, in the tradition of *the pen of my aunt*.

For the linguist the distinction between language as system and language in use is even sharper than might appear from the terminology of "code" versus "message." This basic distinction is more commonly stated in the traditional terminology of "language" versus "speech." These are what the French speak of as *langue* and *parole,* respectively. In this view, even such a specific message as *The pen of my aunt is on the table,* when it is used in a grammar, is not the sentence as it might be used at some specific time and place by some particular speaker. As one of the well-formed sentences of the English language, the "same" sentence might be used by different speakers on different occasions. It would therefore have a multiplicity of possible occurrences. As a sentence constructed according to the rules of English, however, it counts as a single entity, part of language rather than of speech. In fact, if it were never spoken at all, it would still be an English sentence and part of the English language.

If what was said in the previous chapter about the infinity of sentences in natural language is accepted, this follows naturally. For example, the set of natural numbers that have been actually used at least once by English speakers up to the present must be very great indeed; yet this set must also be finite. There is thus an infinity of numbers that have never been used, but which can be made up according to the rules of English and will be understood by English speakers. They belong to the language (*langue*) and thus do not have to have been used in speech (*parole*).

The linguist who is working on a specific language can, of course, make only a finite set of observations. This finite set is commonly called the *corpus;* and it is treated as a sample drawn from an infinite population of sentences. One basic requirement of linguistic theory is that the grammar be such that an infinity of sentences can be constructed by means of rules that are based on a finite corpus.

Thus far, it has been tacitly assumed that the basic subject matter of linguistics as a science is spoken rather than written language. Since language was defined in the previous chapter as including both forms, however, and since my assignment of priority to spoken language reverses the relationship that is current in nonprofessional thinking on the subject, the question plainly calls for further discussion. This issue is closely linked with another one, on which an equally marked difference exists between professional linguists and nonprofessionals—namely, the question of how a norm of correctness for a given language is to be arrived at. The feeling that priority in this respect goes to the written as against the spoken form stems in large part, no doubt, from the belief that the model for linguistic correctness is to be found in the written language.

In accordance with the approach of the first chapter, then, linguistics as the science of language is here taken as embracing both spoken and written forms. Although the primacy of spoken language for linguistics is fundamental, it is reasonable to include both, not only because language as here defined includes both, but also because many problems cannot be dealt with unless the relationship of written to spoken language is taken into account. For example, in instances in which the historical development of a language is being considered, the earlier of two periods is usually represented in written documents.

The priority of spoken language is both phylogenetic and ontogenetic. In the history of the human race, speech exists everywhere and at all times, whereas writing first appeared anywhere long after spoken language, at approximately 3000 B.C. in Egypt. Moreover, even now it has not yet been applied to all spoken languages. There are literally thousands of "unwritten languages," not only those of aboriginal peoples outside the Western and Oriental culture spheres, but also distinct local variants, commonly called dialects, which are found in those areas where standard languages are spoken and yet often differ from the standard language and from each other to the same extent as those forms of speech that are regarded, in preliterate areas, as being different but related languages. A linguist who encountered two speech forms in New Guinea as different as Sicilian and Venetian would probably consider them to be separate languages. Thus many spoken forms existed in the past and still exist in the present without any corresponding written form; every "written" form, however, represents some spoken form. In other words, in specific instances, writing always implies speech, but not vice versa.

Everyone learns to speak before he becomes literate. If his language has no written form, he never of course becomes literate. Even if there is a written form, he may remain illiterate all his life. In fact, until the introduction of universal education during the last two centuries, where writing did exist, it was always the property of a minority of the population. The psychological priority of speech, even among the highly literate minority, is shown by the fact that reading and writing are normally accompanied by auditory and motor imagery, whereas we generally talk without the presence of visual imagery of the written form.

A further consideration of importance for the linguist is the nature of historical change. Linguistic change can be understood in terms of speech change. Writing is not, except in rare and marginal instances, an autonomous source of linguistic change. This can perhaps be most clearly exemplified in sound change. Thus, in a number of languages at different times and places, a $p$ sound has changed to an $f$ sound. This is a relatively small change in articulatory habits. $p$ is a consonant produced by closure of the lips, without vibration of the vocal cords and without nasal resonance. If the closure is not complete, the projecting upper teeth tend to make contact with the lower lip and, since there are spaces between the teeth, we no longer have the momentary stoppage of air characteristic of the $p$ sound. Technically, $p$ is an unvoiced nonnasal bilabial stop and $f$ is an unvoiced nonnasal labiodental spirant. It goes without saying that this change has occurred in various languages independently of whether or not the written symbols resembled each other, or whether in fact the language was written at all. The converse cannot occur. Thus, in the late Aramaic script, the letters for *r* and *d* became identical, yet this produced no merger of the sounds, which are still distinct in the modern forms of Aramaic.

As the result of changes in speech, orthographies eventually cease to have a simple relation to the spoken form. Irregular orthographies are sometimes made the subject of official reform; when this occurs, it is always the written form that is made to conform to the spoken language. Again, an orthographic system may be replaced by official decree with an entirely different one, as when Turkey changed from the Arabic to the Latin alphabet after World War I. Once it was implemented throughout the educational system, this changeover took only a few years. But the psychologically far more deep-rooted system of spoken language cannot be replaced by official decree. This usually takes generations of bilingualism; even then, given the will to resist and the sheer inertia of habit, such change may not ever take place.

It is for reasons such as these that the linguist considers spoken language to be the basic subject of his science. Even when writing systems are subjected to a theoretical analysis parallel to that applied to spoken language, they are not usually analyzed as autonomous systems, but rather in relation to and as representations of the spoken language.

Another basic way in which the views of the professional linguist differ from those of the nonprofessional also has to do with the question of the relative priority of spoken and written language. This is the distinction between descriptive and prescriptive approaches to the study of language—a complex subject, which tends to arouse strong emotions. The professional linguist is as likely to differ on this question, at least on some points, with his colleague who is engaged in the teaching of language and literature as he is with the unsophisticated "man in the street." It must be admitted that the linguist has at times tended to oversimplify the issues at stake and therefore to be as much at fault in this dispute as his "unscientific" opponent.

It may perhaps convey some of the flavor of the dispute if we set up two straw men, extremist advocates of the prescriptive and descriptive points of view, respectively. The fact of the matter is that the straw men in this case are not mere "ideal types"; they can be closely approximated in real life and by actual quotations from the literature on the subject. On the one hand, we have Mr. X, let us say a high school teacher of English, who believes that there is a "correct" or "grammatical" form of English, which is to be found in standard grammars and dictionaries. Unfortunately, the vast majority of his student speakers do not conform to this model; it therefore becomes his business to contribute in a modest way to remedying this situation, by inculcating in his students correct norms of pronunciation, grammar, and vocabulary. These correct usages—for example, to say *It is I* rather than *It is me*, or *He isn't going* instead of *He ain't going*, are not merely matters of arbitrary preference. The favored forms are in some sense more "logical," as when *I* is to be preferred over *me* in *It is I* on the grounds that *I* is "in the nominative case" and thus should be used to designate grammatical subject or any item identical with it. The preference for *isn't* over *ain't* is also likely to be stated in logical terms: The negative of *is* should be *is not* or *isn't*, that of *are* should be *aren't;* the use of the single form *ain't* in the negative destroys the presumably valuable distinction among forms of the verb *to be* that are found in the positive of the verb. In this case, esthetic factors are likely to be invoked also in the accompanying judgment that *ain't* is in some way uglier than *is not*.

The French counterpart of Mr. X, who teaches a language that differs markedly from the local dialects or patois found in various regions outside of Paris, will also no doubt view these usually unwritten forms of speech as inferior, theorizing that they arose as a corruption of the pure French that is enshrined in the French literary language, as based on Parisian speech. If either Mr. X or his French counterpart has thought at all about the unwritten languages spoken by such peoples as American Indians, Africans, or South Sea Islanders, he doubtless thinks of them just as he does of the unwritten dialects of French peasants—as inferior. In fact, in very much the same way as the incorrect forms of English and French fall short of the standard in respect to beauty and logical clarity, so too must such uncultivated tongues be wanting.

At the other extreme is Professor Y, who teaches graduate courses in general linguistic theory. He received his first research support during World War II for writing a practical handbook for the Army to be used by a linguist in conjunction with a native speaker. This was for a language, although a literary language, for which no usable account existed that described its spoken form as it would be encountered by GI's.

Professor Y is emphatic on the subject that linguistics is a *science:* it describes language as it is actually used, and has no scientific basis for preferring one form over another. The speech of a primitive people, of a substandard speaker, of a literary language, of local dialects of a standard language—all are equally good in so far as they fulfill the purposes of communication. Professor Y is likely to quote the great Edward Sapir: "When it comes to linguistic form, Plato walks with the Macedonian swineherd, Confucius with the head-hunting savage of Assam." [1] He will insist on the separateness of linguistics and logic. To the argument that the double negative, such as *I don't see nobody,* cannot be used together to furnish a negative meaning, because two negatives make an affirmative, he will point out that ancient Greek does just that. If Sophocles can say such things as *I don't see nobody nowhere,* how can we reprove a teenager for doing the same thing? Professor Y will point out that the normative grammarian imports extraneous sources of judgment, as when he equates *I* with the Latin nominative and then demands that it be used the same way. He is trying to freeze the language at a particular point in its history. Yet the form he now deifies is itself the product of an historical evolution that he would undoubtedly have opposed at every turn, had he been alive at those times. Modern English is, in a sense, incorrect Anglo-Saxon. As for the esthetic argument, it lacks an objective basis: What we are accustomed to, or what we value for some other reason, elicits a positive esthetic reaction in us; with other values, our esthetic reactions are different. Had Shakespeare been from Brooklyn and written Hamlet in Brooklynese, we would consider the phonetics and grammar of that much-maligned dialect to be the standard of beautiful and correct English. No doubt language teachers, and with them many misguided people whose healthy instincts in these matters have been corrupted by the schools, think that certain forms are more beautiful than others. The linguist takes note of these reactions, but he views them as unfounded, although no doubt a force to be reckoned with. He no more believes that they have a real basis than an ethnologist in Polynesia would believe in the real existence of the native divinities there.

There are, it would seem, a number of logically separate issues in such a debate, but sufficient connection among them so that an individual who takes a particular position on one question is likely also to embrace views on other questions that finally result in something like the "ideologies" sketched above in somewhat exaggerated form. It must be granted that, qua scientist, the linguist should observe what actually occurs, because it is his business to describe and explain this reality. If particular usages are regarded as mere deviations from a correct norm, they will not be described with the fullness and seriousness that they may deserve. But if the normative view tends to disregard altogether certain actual facts, simply because of a predetermined value orientation, the descriptive approach tends to fall down by not specifying in detail the valuational attitudes of speakers toward particular linguistic behavior. If one regards these as merely unfounded beliefs, then of course the details become unimportant. But attitudes toward language are themselves scientific data that, as we shall see, belong strictly speaking to the interdisciplinary areas of psycholinguistics and sociolinguistics. The professional linguist might therefore wish to relegate them to these newly formed hybrids, or to psychology and sociology proper.

This, however, does not seem to be a realistic solution, and for the following reason. Like any other science, linguistics has both a pure and an applied aspect. When the linguist becomes involved in such matters as the standardizing of hitherto unwritten languages for use in the schools, orthographic reform, or the lexical expansion of languages not hitherto employed for technical and scientific purposes, he must inevitably take into account the attitudes of the users of the language on the perils of doctrinaire and unworkable decisions. Even descriptive grammars that are undertaken by linguists with a primarily pure rather than an applied goal are often intended for pedagogical use. It is obviously important that the users of such a grammar, if it includes forms that are considered to be deviations from the norm of cultured speakers, should be informed of that fact. To fulfill their purpose then, pedagogical grammars need to take into account the value judgments of speakers of the language. Further, valuational attitudes are relevant to the linguist, even from the point of view of "pure" rather than applied linguistics. Such attitudes on the part of speakers are, from all appearances, a factor in the spread of speech forms within the community and in their stability over time.

The norm of the professional linguist is, however, descriptive rather than valuational. He is saying, in effect, "If you use the form of the language described in this grammar, you will produce such-and-such reactions on the part of speakers of the language, depending, often enough, on the social position of the speakers themselves." His approach is thus still fundamentally different from that of the normative grammarian. In fact, he might point out that a youth-board worker in a slum area would not be accepted if he did *not* use *ain't* for negation, in all persons and all numbers.

All this does not, or at least should not, imply that, *within* the same speech variety, there are not differences in the use of speech that are susceptible to reasonable value judgment, although the detailed consideration of that matter traditionally belongs to literary studies. Thus, in any form of speech, there can be inexactness and repetitiousness of expression as against effectiveness and economy. On a higher plane, where it becomes difficult to divorce style from content, there may be truly memorable expression, treasured and transmitted by the speech community as a whole and capable of arousing esthetic emotion.

There is still another issue—namely, judgments among varieties in speech of the same language or among different languages. Here again, there may be an objective basis for calling certain forms of speech more cultivated. A dialect that has been used for literary purposes, a language that has clothed the thoughts of great poets or, through gradual "natural" or relatively rapid planned development, has been adapted to scientific or literary uses—such forms of speech do have greater resources for stylistically effective expression. The "democratic" point that can be made legitimately by the linguist is that all dialects and languages begin by being equal, in the sense in which the Declaration of Independence declares all men to have been born equal. But some men have received a college education, essentially through the accidents of history, and any other men who had the same opportunities would probably do as well. So too with languages and their resources—*acquired* resources—for expression. Here, in fact, the literary humanist often turns out to be surprisingly ignorant with regard to the grammatical complexity, lexical richness, and potentialities for literary expression of the languages of preliterate people.

To no people is there lacking the supreme gift of well-formed speech, and there is no language whose structure is not a potential source of esthetic delight.

Having considered the general limits of the subject matter of linguistics and some of its basic value orientations, we now turn to a more detailed consideration of the tasks of linguistic science and of the scientific division of labor that, as may be expected in any science, has grown up in relation to the variety of problems with which the science deals.

Traditionally, the basic division in linguistics has been between the descriptive and the historical branch of the subject. Linguistics in the modern sense is usually regarded as coming into being at the turn of the nineteenth century. The idea that certain resemblances among languages are to be explained in terms of their being the differentiated descendants of a formerly existing language can be traced back to the seventeenth century and even earlier. But it was only in the nineteenth century that the foundations of the comparative-historical method were laid by proceeding to systematic comparisons, as well as to the reconstruction of the ancestral language, particularly in the case of Indo-European. Although many other important linguistic questions had been discussed in earlier periods—as far back at least as the Greeks and Hindus, and not without significant achievement—it was only under the aegis of the comparative-historical method that linguistics developed as an organized discipline, with professorial chairs, journals, and scientific societies.

The comparative-historical orientation remained dominant in linguistics into the first two decades of the twentieth century. During the latter part of that period, there was taking shape a change of revolutionary proportions, which first appeared in systematic form in the posthumous *Cours de linguistique générale* of the Swiss linguist Ferdinand de Saussure.[2] The single general term most frequently employed to characterize the overall trend that, frequently under diverse forms, subsequently came to dominate linguistics both in Europe and the United States is structural-ism. One of its main tenets, as stated by de Saussure, is the distinctness of studies that describe a form of speech at some particular point of time, in abstraction from ongoing change (*synchronic,* in the terminology introduced by de Saussure). This is differentiated from those studies in which synchronic states of different times and places are compared in order to infer changes; these latter studies are called *diachronic.* It is not only that synchronic and diachronic studies are regarded as being distinguishable, one from the other, but that each is considered to be autonomous, and that synchronic studies are of at least equal dignity and importance as diachronic ones. The coherence of synchronic studies rests on the supposition that a synchronic state is an organized system, intelligible in its own terms and without the necessity of reference to its past. This system is con-stituted by the language, *langue* as distinguished from speech in its concrete occurrence, *parole.* This terminology too was introduced into linguistics by de Saussure.

The shift of interest to the internal relations within a language, as against the external comparison of one language with another, received further support from the widening of the horizons of linguistic interest during the twentieth century. Classical comparative-historical linguistics of the nineteenth century was primarily concerned with a single language family, Indo-European, which embraced almost all the languages of Europe and of much of western Asia. There were secondary foci of interest in such families as the Finno-Ugric and the Semitic of the same cultural area, along with a few pioneering applications of the methodology of comparative linguistics to families in other areas that had no extensive earlier written records, chiefly Bantu and Malayo-Polynesian. Largely under the academic aegis of anthropology, although occasioned in large part by the re-quirements of Western missionaries, businessmen, and ad-ministrators, linguistics began to broaden its geographical horizons to include the description of large numbers of non-

Western languages, many of which had not yet received literary codification.

For several reasons, attention tended to be concentrated on synchronic problems. To begin with, the descriptive material that was used by the comparative-historical method was for the most part the language of written texts. The problem of describing hitherto unwritten languages brought into focus many theoretical problems that were involved in description without the aid of already existing texts. Most prominently, such written records implicitly contained a ready-made orthographic analysis of the sound system, which was lacking for unwritten languages. It is no wonder then that problems of the analysis of sound systems bulked so large in the earlier theoretical period of structuralism. Since very few of the languages that were studied had previously been described, the first task was obviously that of description, and on a vast scale, before comparative work could be undertaken. Since these languages usually had no past written records, and not enough descriptive material had been accumulated for comparative study of the level that had been attained in Indo-European studies, the very basis was lacking for understanding and explaining them in terms of past history.

Finally, the descriptivists were faced, in the case of languages such as those of the American Indians, which are remote from our own cultural tradition, with sounds, grammatical systems, and lexicons that differed greatly from those to which investigators had grown accustomed through their studies of Indo-European and other linguistic stocks of Europe and the Near East. Investigation into such languages inevitably raised fundamental theoretical problems with regard to the nature of a satisfactory description of a language and the adequacy of those traditional grammatical categories, based on Western languages, that could largely be taken for granted in the traditional Indo-European studies. All these factors contributed to the shift of theoretical focus from questions of language history to those of language description.

On the basis of these differences in data, methodology, and theoretical interest, the division between descriptive and historical linguistics has tended to persist; a large number, probably a substantial majority of linguists, can now be regarded as specialists in either one or the other.

The synchronic and diachronic specialties that together constitute the core of linguistics as it is actually practiced today are both, in a sense, specific rather than general. This is perhaps more easily seen in diachronic than in synchronic linguistics. Diachronic linguists carry on two main activities. They attempt, to begin with, to reconstruct the history of some particular group of languages and, in that respect, tend to specialize in the study of a single family or even a particular branch of that family—for example, to be Indo-Europeanists or Semitists or Slavicists. Their other activity is theoretical, but it is confined mainly to the discussion of topics that bear more or less directly on the methodological aspects of historical linguistic investigation—for example, the admissibility or nonadmissibility of certain procedures, the basis for judging the validity of rival and incompatible reconstructions, and questions of the terminology to be used in describing changes. Attempts to study changes comparatively, in order to discover their general characteristics as found in many different and historically independent instances, have not played a central role in diachronic linguistics. Instead, the interest has been in the development of an adequate terminology by which to describe and clarify changes rather than to generalize with regard to these changes.

*Mutatis mutandis,* the same things have held true for descriptive linguistics. The bulk of the work that has been carried on by descriptive linguistics has been of two types, very much like those enumerated above for historical-comparative linguistics: the production of actual linguistic descriptions (grammars, dictionaries, and so forth) and theoretical discussions about the requirements for an adequate description. Obviously such descriptive work, as well as the elaboration of a theoretical framework within which it can be carried out, are among the prerequisites for comparisons that are directed toward generalization, but they do not take the place of the generalizing activity itself. The term *panchronic* has been proposed for such studies; in more recent discussions, however, the topic has been dealt with under the title of *universals*. Most of this book will be taken up with an examination of these chief areas of linguistics proper: those of synchronic, diachronic, and generalizing studies.

# III

# DESCRIPTIVE LINGUISTICS

Comparative studies by definition presuppose the existence of objects to be compared. In linguistics, these are the individual "languages," whose description almost always takes the form of grammars and dictionaries. Each of these descriptions is customarily labeled by the name of a language and by an indication of the approximate time span for which the description is meant to be valid. Let us call the object of such a description a *language state*. There then arise, at the very threshold of scientific linguistics, a series of questions that can be classified into three types.

The first question has to do with the meaning of *language* in the term *language state*. Linguistic description is usually derived from a relatively small number of informants, yet it always claims to be more than an account of the speech of these particular individuals. The grammar or dictionary that is produced is supposed to be in some way representative of a language—that is to say, of a characteristic cultural institution of a social group. The second series of questions has to do with the meaning of *state* in the phrase *language state.* How can a description refer to a specific time when, like all other social institutions, language is in a perpetual process of change? The third group of questions has to do with the relation between the primary data of recorded utterances and the grammar of lexicon that purports to describe them. How are scientific conditions of adequacy to be laid down for such a description?

We may illustrate the kind of question that arises in this last connection by referring to our earlier discussion regarding the infinity of natural language and the distinction between language as a system (*langue*) and its concrete utilization (*parole*). Linguistics, which was marked off from other sciences by its concern with system rather than with use, must therefore have a theory for the production of grammars of specific language states that will include rules to govern the formation of an infinity of sentences based, however, on the necessarily finite set of utterances that the linguist records in his work with informants. This body of materials is commonly called, as we noted earlier, the corpus.

We now turn to our first problem, the locus of the term *language,* when it is used as a label for a particular linguistic description. The linguist, seeking a purely linguistic criterion for a "language," usually defines it in terms of potential mutual intelligibility. The employment of this criterion reflects a sound instinct; it seeks to deal with the question about the degree of similarity that is necessary in order for different speech forms to constitute variants of the same language, by attempting to answer it in terms of the possibilities of social interaction. Mutual intelligibility, however, turns out to be highly variable; it depends, in borderline cases, on individual intelligence, on past experience with dialect variations, and even on emotionally conditioned intergroup attitudes. In practice, the linguist follows the social consensus on such matters, a consensus which, to be sure, always has a linguistic basis, but yet is inextricably involved with nonlinguistic factors. Thus speech forms that, viewed objectively, may have roughly the same degree of similarity, are considered by the speakers of these forms to be separate languages if politically distinct tribal communities are involved—for example, in New Guinea—but to be dialects of the same language if the speakers share a common literary norm and affiliations to the same national political unit—for example, in Europe. Yet linguistic realities also play a role. Thus, under no circumstances would Basque be regarded as a dialectal form of French.

This implies that every language community is marked by linguistic variability, to a greater or lesser degree. Until now, by far the most potent variable in the production of intralinguistic differences has been geographical location. Every speech community of any considerable geographical extension comprises local variants known as *dialects*. Potentially, however, any socially isolating mechanism may be the source for differing forms of speech within the same overall speech community. Among the bases for such linguistic differentiation are class, religious affiliation, industrial occupation, and sex. Insofar as any of these exhibits a systematic linguistic nature, we may extend the notion of dialect proper, applied *par excellence* to local dialect, and speak of class, religious, or occupational dialects.

On the assumption that every individual has some peculiarities of speech that distinguish him from all other speakers of the same language, the term *idiolect* has been used to designate individual speech systems. We thus have a sequence of concepts: idiolect, individual speech, dialect, the speech of a linguistically distinguishable set of speakers roughly congruent with some group defined in nonlinguistic terms, and, most inclusively, the total language community.

Such an analysis does not appear to do justice, however, to the real complexities of the situation. The notion of idiolect, for example, has never been clarified in respect to its two possible interpretations. Granted as at least possible that the speech of every individual is distinguishable in some fashion from that of every other individual, on one interpretation the individual has one or more completely idiosyncratic traits that are not found in any other speaker. On the other hand, perhaps there are no such traits; instead every individual speaker has a unique combination of features, each one of which, taken singly, is found in at least one other speaker.

Since dialect can reasonably be defined as the existence of a set of unique traits, on the first view the idiolect is a dialect that has one speaker, while what are usually called dialects are collections of these that share traits which are common to all members of the dialect-speaking group, but are not found in any other dialect. On the second view, the difference between idiolect and dialect is logically basic: while a dialect has unique common characteristics, an idiolect does not.

Without choosing among these alternatives, we may point to still more serious considerations, which would suggest that, while the idiolect, in the sense of the speech of an individual, arises out of the experience of the field linguist in his work with a single informant and therefore exists at the level of primary data, it is in fact internally heterogeneous, so that it actually requires analysis in terms of several simultaneous or successive norms. Thus, certain aspects of an individual's speech may undergo modification in accordance with temporary group affiliations (for example, boarding school or the army), or with more permanent shifts (for example, as the result of migration to another geographically defined dialect area or of change in class status). Further, every individual seems to vary his speech in accordance with situational variables. Such variations have sometimes been called stylistic, and among the terms that are commonly used to designate styles are "colloquial," "intimate," "formal," and so forth. Most of our information about variation on this level is contained in those linguistic descriptions that distinguish, no doubt in oversimplified fashion, two polar types: *lento*, which is marked by slower speech tempo and greater care in enunciation, as opposed to the more rapid and less careful *allegro* style.

This suggests that the individual's speech owes its uniqueness to the particular intersection of temporary and permanent group affiliations, whose configuration is in each case, to begin with, an historical product of his life history, further crosscut by situational stylistic variants. This configuration probably contains, in addition, certain fully idiosyncratic traits, which are a result of the individual's particular personality and life history. Hence individual speech, instead of constituting an integral object of description, is rather to be understood as a complex, whose elements must be isolated by reference to the speech of other individuals.

From available evidence, probably the most that can be asserted with reasonable confidence is that speech communities display highly complex patterns of internal variation, along the lines sketched here and possibly along others. In spite of recently heightened interest in such matters, as is indicated by the appearance and growth of sociolinguistics as a quasi-independent field of investigation, we lack data, except for selected parameters in certain individual cases; even here, existing studies involve casual rather than systematic sampling of the universe under investigation.

The one conspicuous exception is that, for certain areas, systematic investigation of variation by locality does exist, in the form of dialect atlases. These constitute a well-established branch of linguistic investigation, until recently dominated by purely historical interests, however, so that old informants, with the locally "most genuine" and archaic speech, were sought out rather than a representative sample of each community.

It is evident that the descriptive linguist, as a matter of practical expediency—if he is not to devote all his energies to the study of variations that are internal to the speech community—must restrict his investigation to a small number of individual informants. These may be regarded as a sample of the speech community; yet, in the absence of basic information about community variation, the sample is not random but haphazard, and we do not know for certain of what it is actually representative.

With the putative future growth of sociolinguistics, it may become possible to approach the problem with some approximation to what a sociologist would regard as at least the most elementary consideration of sampling. Until now, there has been relatively little awareness of the problem, so that the necessary techniques and the analytical framework for such investigations are still in the pioneer stage. It is probably a fair statement of the actual situation to say that informants are chosen at best in terms of some priority, in the form of their command of the most widespread and socially acceptable dialect, and are maintained on the basis of qualities that have nothing to do with the requirements of a representative sample of the speech community—for example, intelligence, patience, a spontaneous interest in the work, and a personality concordant with that of the investigator.

Nevertheless, there are some mitigating circumstances that have enabled descriptive linguists to produce scientifically usable descriptions, in spite of their almost sovereign disregard of these problems. Language is probably the most standardized aspect of human culture. In the perspective of the total structure, the extent of variation, at least within a locally defined dialect, is modest. As a consequence, even a small, unspecified sample will provide reliable evidence of those basic attributes of linguistic structure that are of chief interest to the linguist. Furthermore, in regard to the most basic cleavage in the speech community—that which occurs along the lines of local dialects—speakers of the language can usually provide reasonably reliable information so that, even without any elaborate sociolinguistic investigation, the linguist can identify these dialects and investigate their chief points of difference.

We now turn to a consideration of the problem of

chronological placement of a description. Although the basic issue is a general scientific one, the method of dealing with it varies according to the particular science. All linguistic description is built on observations that necessarily range over an appreciable period of time, during which the object of the description is itself undergoing changes. In spite of this, synchronic studies are made in which the object of the description is treated as an entity for which abstraction has been made from the processes of change. Indeed, the study of change itself in linguistics proceeds from the comparison of such timeless state descriptions, under circumstances in which the chronological separation is sufficiently broad to permit significant differences to be noted.

Certain characteristics of the normal course of change in language will indicate how synchronic descriptions can be carried out that will successfully capture the scientifically relevant aspects of linguistic structure. At the same time, the existence of ongoing change appears in certain features of the description.

One important factor that facilitates linguistic description is the relatively slow rate of change in the case of language. The bulk of vocabulary, grammatical rules, and phonetic characteristics are not susceptible to detectable change during such periods as are usually devoted to the study of a language by a particular investigator. No language changes so fast that grandparents cannot understand their grandchildren; in fact, that situation is not even approached. The overriding need for communication within a given linguistic community ordinarily prevents change from being so rapid as to result in the loss of effective social cooperation by means of a common language.

Furthermore, change in language is never instantaneous. For example, if a change occurs in a sound system, as the result of which all $p$ sounds are replaced by $f$—a change that, when it is completed, would be stated in the formula $p > f$, it is not possible to specify a time $t_1$ such that all speakers before $t_1$ used $p$ and all after $t_1$ used $f$. In fact, the linguistic heterogeneity of the speech community, which was discussed earlier in this chapter, is essentially a resultant of the noninstantaneousness of linguistic change and in turn perpetuates it. A change that is initiated in some dialectal subgroup of the language community will, for a number of reasons, usually tend to spread more easily within the dialect than across dialect boundaries. For one thing, the greater uniformity of linguistic structure within the dialect facilitates the adoption of linguistic innovations. Speakers of the same dialect are in more intensive contact if the original communication situation that gave rise to the existing divisions persists. Besides, agreement in speaking the same dialect is likely to be a factor in the formation of other social groupings, whose existence then reinforces the predominance of intradialectal communication.

At a particular time, then, during which such a change as $p > f$ is in progress, we would expect to find that, in certain sectors of the speech community, the change has already been completed and only $f$ is used, while in other sectors it is still in the process of accomplishment. Where the latter holds true, perhaps some individuals have only $f$, and some have the earlier $p$, while others—perhaps the majority—have alternative pronunciations for some or all pairs of words with original $p$ and innovative $f$. We may hypothesize that the relative frequency of the competing forms in individuals is a measure of the extent to which the change has been accomplished in individual cases. For certain kinds of changes, particularly those in the sound system, such variants show relevant differences even with the individual's speech. Typically, the innovation first appears in the *allegro* or less formal style, and only later invades the more formal or *lento* style.

We have already referred to groups within which the change has been fully accomplished, and those in which it is in the process of being accomplished. There may also be groups within which the change has not yet made its appearance. Insofar as, in some instances, it may never become established in these subdivisions of the speech community, what happens is that a dialect difference is initiated or an old one still further accentuated. Indeed, this is the mechanism by which dialects become more and more divergent, until they reach the condition of being separate but related languages.

From the vantage point of the speech of the individual, then, the phenomenon of ongoing change should be reflected in the existence of functionally equivalent forms, known technically as *free variants*, either within the same style or between styles. In fact, such free variation is a recurrent element in synchronic descriptions; it serves as an indication of a change that is in progress. One of the competing forms is the older, the other the more recent. When the speech of an informant is studied over a period of time, what is detected as changing is the relative frequency of these alternative forms. It is the normal practice of descriptivists merely to note the alternation, without carrying through the difficult task of specifying relative frequency, although sometimes one alternative is stated to be more frequent or even much more frequent than the other. The triumph of the innovating form is by no means inevitable: Sometimes the older form reasserts itself, while slang passes in and out of the language, generally without becoming established. Sometimes two forms exist side by side, by developing distinct functions. For example, English *shade* and *shadow* are different case forms of the same Anglo-Saxon word, and, prior to the collapse of the case system in English, had the same lexical meaning. Originally free variants with the same meaning, they later developed the difference of meaning that served to perpetuate them as distinct forms.

Even though a description departs from usual practice, it gains in theoretical significance if the purely static approach is abandoned and the free variants are specified in terms of older form and innovating form, an identification that can usually be established from a variety of evidence. In that way, the distribution of the two forms in the wider community can be dealt with from a dynamic point of view.

Not all changes entail replacement. Some innovations, particularly in vocabulary, are incremental, in that they add to, rather than replace, the existing reservoir of forms. Others are decremental, in that the older forms are in the process of being lost without replacement. These processes are most obvious in technological vocabulary. Here again the changes are to be conceived of as taking place by stages within a heterogeneous speech community, and as being reflected in changes of frequency over time.[1]

The two sets of problems that have been discussed up to now both refer to external connections of the corpus— namely, its temporal and spatial placement. We now turn to the more internal question of the relationship between the corpus itself and the linguistic description that is based upon it. Theoretical discussion of this relationship apparently has two aspects. One has to do more closely with the relationship of the description to the corpus. Are there, in the relationship between the corpus as evidence and the finished product, any constancies that reflect statable and theoretically defensible general principles? The other aspect has to do with the nature of the descriptions themselves. Here too generalizability is evidently a desideratum. The scientific study of language requires that our descriptions be so constructed that the objects they describe become comparable.

Our initial discussion of the conformity of natural languages already contained some implications for the relation between corpus and description. Since the corpus, which consists of the actual utterances recorded by the linguist, is necessarily finite, and the description that he writes must also be finite, it follows that the grammar must contain mechanisms for producing an infinity of sentences, an infinite subset of which did not occur in the corpus. We see then that the simplest possible relation between corpus and description—namely, for the description to be merely an enumeration of the contents of the corpus—is inadequate.

We have just observed that a grammar should be able to account for sentences that are not in the corpus. One might have thought that every sentence in the corpus would be produced by the grammar. Here again, however, the relationship is a complex one. If by the corpus we mean the set of actual utterances in all their physical detail, then the point made in our previous discussion becomes relevant— namely, that the relationship between a sentence as the kind of object that belongs to the language (*langue*) and an actual occurrence in speech (*parole*) is that between type and token. The corpus consists of such speech tokens. If the same sentence of the language has multiple occurrences in the corpus, however, these will never be exactly the same as a succession of physical events. When a speaker of a language is asked to repeat a sentence, there are generally differences in the two renditions, yet the speaker, as well as any other member of the speech community, will usually agree that these are two different instances (tokens) of the same sentence (type), rather than two different sentences.

A comparison with music may be useful here. If two musicians play the same composition, or even if the same musician performs it on different occasions, there will be differences in tempo, phrasing and dynamics. In spite of this, we say that these were different performances of the same composition rather than different compositions. In just the same way, variations in language in regard to certain characteristics, such as speech tempo, and the occurrence and duration of pauses, are regarded as being peculiar to the specific performance. The parallel goes even further. Mistakes in execution do not invalidate a particular performance as being that of the musical work in question, nor do they change the score. So too, slips of the tongue and similar errors of performance in speech are generally taken as tokens of the sentences in their correct form, rather than in the form in which they actually occurred in speech.

In one important respect, however, the task of the linguist is more difficult than that of the music critic: he does not start with a score; it is his task to construct the linguistic equivalent of a score from the performances that constitute the corpus.

Drastic editing of the corpus is required in some cases: False starts, repetitions, aposiopeses, changes of construction in midstream, subordinate clauses given main clause status and thus forming apparent sentences in isolation— none of these are taken at their face value. The language is therefore a kind of ideal object, like many other objects in scientific theory, such as frictionless bodies, perfect vacuums, and so forth.

All this may seem to be so self-evident that it does not require discussion. The fact is that all schools of linguistics, however empiricist they have claimed to be, have edited the corpus along the lines just described. Indeed, the question has hardly been discussed until recently, presumably because the linguist, like other speakers, has learned, during the course of acquiring his own language, to abstract from certain variations that are irrelevant to the message and thus to edit and correct unconsciously what he hears. When he describes his own or another language scientifically, he subjects the new data to an interpretation that is based on his established, although usually nonverbalized, practice in these matters.

In spite of this agreement in practice and virtual self-evidence, it is clearly part of the task of a general theory of linguistic description to provide a reasoned basis for the various ways in which the corpus is interpreted as evidence for the language system. In so doing, such a theory does not reject observation; rather, it extends the frame of observation beyond that of the pure sound itself to other aspects of the situation, including its systematic semantic interpretation and the metalinguistic reactions of the speaker, as when he corrects himself. No attention is paid to differences that are observed to be only randomly related to the message.

Often it is membership of these events in other behavioral systems that leads to the making of this decision without systematic observation of their relation to the message content. Thus interruptions by coughing are related to the overall condition of the speaker when he is not speaking, as well as to their absence in other speakers; they are thus attributed to a different behavioral system and judged to be irrelevant to the message. General considerations lead us to believe that the situation in all speech communities is by and large the same in such matters, but on this question we are always open to correction by observation. Thus, if we noted in some previously uninvestigated language that all the speakers coughed just once in most sentences, we would suspect some relevance to the message. If it turned out on further observation that the nominal subject of a main clause was always preceded by a cough, that fact would be incorporated in the grammar. (No such cases, of course, have been reported.)

The type-token distinction has a still further consequence for linguistic description. Frequency of occurrence of sentences will be irrelevant: either a sentence is part of the language or it is not. A frequency of zero in the corpus —that is, its nonoccurrence—is merely a mathematically limiting case. Description draws no distinction between those sentences, formed in accordance with its rules, that happen to be represented in the corpus and those that are not; among those that do occur, frequency of occurrence is irrelevant since it refers to the token, not the type.

If, however, we consider the frequency not of sentences but of shorter items that appear in many different sentences—for example, phonemes, words or word classes —these often exhibit systematic characteristics such as may be shown to have an important relationship to universal characteristics of language structure and hence to have theoretical significance. For example, where nouns have a singular/plural distinction, the evidence thus far indicates that singulars are generally about four or five times as frequent as plurals. Such differences in relative frequency will later be shown to be plausibly connected with purely structural characteristics. This does not mean that we need to modify our conception of an adequate language description if it is logically coherent, agrees with the usual practice of linguists, and is theoretically fruitful.

It is simply that the production of language descriptions is not the only task of descriptive linguistics or of linguistics in general. The linguist must be willing to undertake other kinds of studies, where they promise to be of relevance to the understanding of his primary object of inquiry. Certain phenomena, which are rightly excluded from linguistic description on the grounds that they are characteristic solely of performance, may be studied in their own right. For example, slips of the tongue are in many respects not random; while they may be irrelevant to the content of the specific messages in which they occur, they shed light on the process of language change, as well as on some of the psychological aspects of speech performance. Further, pauses are related in certain ways to syntactic structure and for that reason are worthy of investigation.

Certain guiding principles that are part of general scientific methodology need to be considered in their specific application to a theory of linguistic description. While such concepts as simplicity and completeness have probably never received sufficiently precise formulation in discussions of scientific methodology, their importance in scientific practice is undeniable. One overriding principle is accuracy, by which is meant conformity to the facts of the language. Thus, a description is inadequate if sentences may be produced by its rules that are not acceptable to speakers as part of the language; a general theory derived in accordance with such rules for specific languages must be seriously wrong. Just how we may know that a specific sentence belongs to the language is the problem of grammaticality. The obverse of accuracy is completeness. Not only should everything that is produced by the grammar belong to the language, but everything that belongs to the language must be capable of being produced by the grammar. Since, as we have seen, every natural language consists of an infinite set of sentences, strictly speaking, we can never know if it is complete. For a living language, the corpus, while finite, is expandable; completeness may therefore be tested by the ability to account for sentences that occur subsequently. Failure in this respect leads to emendation of the description, and that way completeness may be more and more closely approximated.

The requirements just mentioned, while they are basic, are clearly not sufficient. We expect more of a scientific description than merely accuracy and an approximation to completeness. A large part of what we look for comes under the head of generalization. Thus an account of the plural formation of nouns in English that ran something like this— the plural of *hat* is *hats;* the plural of *coat* is *coats;* the plural of *hand* is *hands,* and so on, enumerating every plural individually—might be accurate and complete; a general rule, however, which first enumerates the special, "irregular plurals," such as *man/men* and then gives a single general rule for ——*s* plurals is clearly superior. Above all, such a set of rules will be much shorter. This requirement has often been stated in terms of simplicity, and the criterion that has sometimes been suggested for judging the relative simplicity of descriptions is their length, as measured by the number of symbols used. While this may be valuable heuristically, I believe that the primary notion is generalizing power in terms of scope (e.g., the ——*s* plural rule covers a very large number of cases), while simplicity and brevity are important consequences.

We might also require a certain kind of "insightfulness," in that a scientific description should reveal relationships in the phenomena studied—for example, it should not merely give rules that are sufficient to produce both active and passive sentences in English, but should also show how a group of active sentences of a specified structure is related to the corresponding passive set. It might be argued that such insights are in principle another facet of generality.

We still have to consider the implications for descriptive theory of another general feature of linguistic systems, as distinguished from other kinds of communication—namely, duality, the existence of two levels, at one of which the elements, like the letters of the alphabet in written language, are individually meaningless, while at the other, the functioning units, like the words of language, are individually meaningful. In spoken language, in accordance with this division, we can distinguish phonology, the study of sound systems, from the remainder of the description.

Indeed, the sound system of a language seems to involve a practically autonomous set of habits of articulation and perception. In learning a foreign language, some speakers "acquire" a satisfactory grasp of its grammatical structure and vocabulary, and even become fluent in it without ever changing the basis of their articulation from that employed in their first language. While classical scholars may develop a strong feeling for the niceties of the grammatical structure of Greek, which they then put to use in textual emendation and interpretation, it is fair to say that, if by some miracle they were dropped down in ancient Athens, because of their pronunciation they would not be able either to obtain or to understand directions on how to get to the Agora. The opposite case is that of the linguist trained in phonetics who can often convincingly reproduce the sounds of a language without more than a rudimentary knowledge of its grammar or vocabulary.

We may thus isolate phonology as a largely autonomous aspect of descriptive linguistics. Its distinctiveness is unquestionable and must be taken into account in any overall theory of descriptive linguistics.

Another separable area is that of lexicon. This is shown in traditional descriptions by the fact that a separate kind of production, the dictionary, is devoted to this part of language descriptions. Again, there seems to be a difference in the skills involved in this acquisition. In learning a foreign language, one could master the grammatical structure with but limited vocabulary resources, and vice versa.

There is evidently a third principal division of language description, grammar. This seems far more difficult to characterize than phonology, with its direct reference to sound, or lexicon, with its reasonably clear-cut defining of the application of specific "meaningful" sound sequences—for example, *table* in English—by reference to facts that are external to language. Conventional grammars appear to consist of a heterogeneous assortment of "rules," for example, of word order; quasi-philosophical definitions, for example, of "noun"; and tables of declension and conjugation.

Nevertheless, we may isolate certain specific topics as typically grammatical, if we consider once again the task faced by an individual who is learning a foreign language. If he is to translate a specific sentence into the foreign language, he cannot merely use the translation equivalent for each item, pronouncing it in accordance with the rules of the phonology. The manner in which these elements are organized differs from language to language, and has always seemed to the professional linguists to be the very heart of linguistic description. Thus, in translating a sentence that contains the phrase *the white house* into French, one must know that the French equivalent of *white* follows the equivalent of *house*, and does not precede it, as in English. Rules for the order of meaningful elements are typically grammatical facts, and, in order to state such a rule in its generality, we must delimit the classes of nouns and adjectives in English and French. Such class concepts are peculiarly grammatical. Again, in order to translate correctly we must choose between *le* and *la* for *the* and *blanc* and *blanche* for *white*. These choices cannot be made from any knowledge of the lexical meaning of *the* or *white* but are based on the understanding of the two-gender system of French nouns. It may be convenient for the dictionary to give us the information that *maison* (house) is feminine, but the ability to make use of this information derives from an understanding of the gender system of French—a grammatical fact *par excellence*.

We shall see later that the boundary between lexicology and grammar is by no means clear-cut in all instances. For present purposes, it is sufficient to point to the existence of three main aspects of description: phonology, grammar, and lexicon. This is a basic fact with which all descriptive theories must somehow deal, and a large part of the distinctiveness of particular theories rests on how the border regions are apportioned and how their interrelationships are conceived.

# IV

## GRAMMATICAL THEORY

The two characteristic products of grammatical description have traditionally been the grammar and the lexicon. Since the chief usefulness of a dictionary is that it enables one to "look up" the meaning of unfamiliar items (normally "words") and since, whatever else a dictionary may also contain, it always includes definitions, one might conclude that the distinction between lexicon and grammar coincides with the distinction between the semantic and the nonsemantic aspects of language.

Examination of both grammars and dictionaries, however, shows that this division is not usually maintained: There are significant exceptions to it from both sides. Thus, as appears most conspicuously in dictionaries of such highly inflected languages as Latin, lexicons generally supply information about the inflectional class membership of individual entries, an indisputably grammatical fact. On the other hand, since the dictionary lists separate items, it does not undertake the semantic task of sentence interpretation. Whatever we do learn in a systematic way from language description as to how the grammatical meaning of higher-level units is related to the "lexical" meaning of individual language elements, is contained, at least in traditional treatments, in the grammar.

A little reflection will show that these exceptions from both sides have a systematic basis. The demarcation of grammar from lexicon rests on something other than the division between the semantic and nonsemantic aspects of language. Grammar is the realm of general rules; lexicon, that of particular elements. Thus, in Latin, that every noun whose nominative singular ends in *-a* has a genitive singular ending in *-ae*, is a rule that, along with many other rules of a similar character, is contained succinctly in the paradigms of the grammar. No Latin grammar, however, contains a complete listing of the membership of the class of nouns (the traditional first declension) that have a nominative singular ending in *-a* and a genitive singular ending in *-ae*. Information of that sort is contained in the lexicon, which gives the declensional class membership of each noun it lists. The individual "meanings" that are stated in the form of definitions or translation equivalents, with an assist from diagrams and pictures, are precisely the most irreducibly individual facts of language: they are not, in general, deducible from any rule or from the meaning of any other item. Knowing that *bouche* in French means *mouth* does not help me in any way to discover that *cheveux* means *hair*.

Some words are "analyzable," to be sure, in the sense that they are made up of smaller items in some regular way, by compounding or by derivation from elements that recur either in isolation or in other combinations. Thus the English word *poetess* can be "guessed" to mean female poet. This only demonstrates once again the validity of the basis suggested here for the distinction between lexicon and grammar. In conventional grammars, the section on "word formation" will give the rules for such derivational affixes as *-ess*. Given these rules and the lexical meaning of *poet*, we may be able to derive the meaning of *poetess,* so that a separate lexical entry for the latter may not seem necessary. In that sense, the meaning of *poetess* is "deducible" from other information, but this does not work in the other direction. Since *-ess* cannot be added freely to any isolated noun —for example, to form *engineeress* or *kingess,* it is a particular fact, discoverable from the lexicon, that the combination *poetess* is part of English, while in other cases the result of using *-ess* as a suffix may produce non-English.

In the light of the fact that grammars are concerned with rules—that is, with generalizing descriptive statements, while lexicons have to do with particulars, it is not surprising that the part of linguistic theory that has to do with descriptive linguistics is mainly concerned with the theory of grammar rather than that of the lexicon. As a result, the theory of lexicography has been largely neglected in linguistics. In regard to the main activity of the lexicographer, the preparation of definitions—the theoretical side—has been for the most part left to the logicians, who do not focus on the problems of definition in empirically given natural languages; the practical side, on the other hand, has been left to the lexicographers, who often develop admirable skill in such matters with a minimum theoretical basis. In this respect, lexicography can indeed be considered an art, or rather, since its esthetic content is relatively insignificant, a technique. There are signs, however, that this long period of theoretical neglect, along with the separation of lexicography from the theoretical mainstream of linguistics, is drawing to a close.[1]

In the present chapter, we shall be concerned with some theoretical models, of varying degrees of explicitness, that have served as organizing principles for grammatical description. Since, as we have seen, those aspects of linguistic description that involve generalizing statements have been the province of grammars rather than of lexicons, theoretical discussions of descriptive theory have tended to be virtually identical with those of grammatical theory, although the place of lexicography within the province of description may sometimes become an important question.

A very large number of grammars of individual languages exist; of these, the great majority have been written with a minimum of explicit statement on theoretical matters. Yet examination of this body of traditionally oriented grammars shows a reasonably coherent underlying model, which is affiliated most closely with the descriptive theory that was evolved in the grammatical tradition of the Greeks and Romans and thereafter employed in the teaching of English and other languages. No one undertakes to write a grammar from scratch. Even the missionary or government official who is untrained in linguistics but has some practical command of a language other than English inevitably produces a grammar that is conditioned either by the traditional language teaching that he has received during the course of his own education, or by direct imitation of the organization of other grammars he has seen. This method of writing grammars has been characterized as the "word paradigm" model. It will be discussed in some detail here, since its basic assumptions underlie much popular thinking about language and the emergence of structural linguistics is to be understood in large part as a reaction against the weaknesses of this traditional model. In turn, the newly developing transformational approach, itself a reaction against certain aspects of structural linguistics, tends to find some points of contact with the earlier model.

Scientific linguistics in its modern form arose at the turn of the nineteenth century, in connection with historical problems. Throughout the nineteenth century, it centered around problems of genetic classification and comparative reconstruction, particularly with regard to the Indo-European family of languages, to which the great majority of the languages of Western Europe belonged. In order to compare languages, it is necessary first to have descriptive data concerning them in the form of grammars and dictionaries. For

the Indo-European comparatist, the languages most necessary for his work were the older forms of the literary languages of the Indo-European stock, such as Latin, Greek,
and Sanskrit. For these he possessed descriptions that were
ultimately based on models developed by Classic and Indian
grammarians, in reasonable accord with the specific structural peculiarities of those languages. They thus proved to
be on the whole satisfactory for the requirements of the
comparative linguist; when the need arose to construct grammars for other older Indo-European languages, these same
models were adapted to the task in hand—for example, the
writing of grammars for such languages as Gothic, Old
Church Slavonic, and Avestan.

During this same period, grammars—chiefly of two
types—were of course also written for modern languages.
One type comprised written languages, in their standardized literary form. Indeed, the grammars for these languages
were frequently conceived of as efforts toward standardization. The development of these literary languages was an
important element in the formation of the nationalisms that
arose in Europe during the nineteenth century. It invested
the ethnic group with a sense of dignity based on its possession of a literary norm and provided a supraregional
standard that played a significant role in transcending particularistic loyalties that were rooted in local group identity.
The other type of contemporary language description was
one outcome of missionary and governmental activities in
non-Western areas; it was dominated by the practical aim
of imparting knowledge of these languages to people who
would be needing them in their administrative, proselytizing,
or commercial activity. Grammars of this sort, except for
occasional and usually inessential deviations, followed the
same general pattern of the "word paradigm" model.

The fundamental concept underlying this model is that
of the word; on that basis, grammar has two fundamental
divisions. One of these is morphology, which is concerned
with the internal structure of the word—for example, word

formation (compounding, derivation) and inflection. The
other is syntax, which describes the rules by which words
are combined to form a sentence.

This notion of "word" is, however, ambiguous in at least
one respect. In many instances—for example, in the case of
classes of inflected words, such as the verb in English—
there are series of related forms that are commonly regarded
as instances of the same word—for example, *sing/sang/sung*,
although in certain contexts one may speak of the word
*sing*. It is such paradigm sets that are the fundamental units
of this grammatical model.

In order to avoid ambiguity in the present discussion, I
shall use the term *lexeme* for paradigm sets and the term
*word* for their individual members. It is customary to use
some agreed-on member of the paradigm set as a "citation"
form for the paradigm—for example, in English, the singular
nonpossessive form for the noun. Thus, in the present context, the lexeme *man* will be the citation for the set *man/
man's/men/men's*, while the word *man* will stand for the
first element of that set.

Lexemes are thus fundamental in a number of ways that
are related to the morphology-syntax division referred to
previously. Thus, in regard to semantics, the dictionary is a
list of lexemes, each represented in its citation form. Hence,
the dictionary entry *man* embraces the paradigm *man/
man's/men/men's*. These are assumed to have a common
root meaning as defined in the dictionary. On the other
hand, the difference of meaning between *man* and *men* is
not dealt with in the dictionary. Each inflected word of the
same paradigm belongs to one of a limited set of inflected
categories—for example, singular, plural, past, present—
whose role in the semantic interpretation of the sentence is
described in the grammar rather than in the dictionary.

Thus the notion of an inflectional set involves a theory
of two kinds of meaning. What is common to a paradigm set
is lexical meaning, which is stated in the dictionary and
viewed as basically constant in all the inflected forms. The

fact that the same lexeme may be subject to different interpretations in different verbal contexts was taken care of by the notion of "polysemy"—that is, the vast majority of lexical entries have a multiplicity of meanings, each of which constitutes a subentry. It then devolves upon the user of the dictionary to choose the particular meaning that is appropriate to the context in which it is being used. How different meanings must be to be regarded as separate homonymous lexical entries, rather than as varieties of the same polysemous lexeme, was never shown satisfactorily.

By contrast with the inherently nonrelational lexical meaning, the meaning of an inflectional category involves a relationship among words in a sentence. The most general types of such relationships are subsumed under such terms as "agreement," as when an adjective "agrees with" a noun in gender, or "government," as when a particular preposition in German is said to "govern" the dative case. Such matters as these are, of course, treated in the grammar rather than in the lexicon.

The main task of morphology is to provide systematic rules in accordance with which the paradigm set of any lexeme can be derived. The lexemes are classified into sets within which the paradigm can be derived by the same rules. There are the well-known declensional and conjugational classes of traditional grammar. For example, the "first" declension of nouns in Latin includes all nouns that have a nominative singular ending in -*a*. All these nouns follow the same declensional pattern in that they end in -*ae* in the genitive and dative singular and nominative plural, -*ā* in the ablative singular, and so on. Usually one particular lexeme is chosen—for example, *puell-a* (girl) in the first declension —and any other first declension noun can then be declined by using it as a model or example (paradigm < Greek *paradeigma* [an example]).

Since the use of the particular inflectional category— that is, its role in the overall semantic interpretation of the sentence—is part of syntax, and the lexical meaning of each

lexeme is in the dictionary, the morphological part of grammar may be viewed as purely formal (morphology < Greek
*morphologia* [study of form]).

Many words in all languages, and all or almost all words
in a few languages, are indeclinable. This means that the
paradigm set consists of only a single word; hence, exten-
sionally, the lexeme and the word are identical. For the
ancient and modern European languages with which the
comparatist had to deal, however, there were numerous inflected lexemes, and their analysis into declensional and conjugational sets was a complex matter. This analysis therefore
tended to form the core of grammar, in the sense that it
seemed to be the most indispensable part. In actual fact, it
took up more space than any other topic; all the other types
were more or less slighted—for example, phonology and
syntax.

As central and important as it was, however, inflection
did not necessarily constitute the sole subject matter of
morphology. The Indian grammatical tradition, with its careful treatment of word formation, in general differed somewhat from the Classical grammarian's emphasis on inflection. With regard to such an English word as *poetesses*, it
seemed to be a systematic part of morphology, interpreted
as word formation, to include a rule by which the fact could
be established that the word *poetesses* is the plural nonpossessive member of the lexeme *poetess*. It also seemed in
order to show that the relationship between *poetess* and
*poet* is the same as that between *authoress* and *author*.
Nevertheless, the employment of suffixes as *-ess* was subject
to apparently capricious restrictions (e.g., *duchess*, but not
*kingess*), which could be more conveniently assigned to the
lexicon. Furthermore, semantic interpretation was not regular in the same way as inflectional categories were.

Thus, if in Latin, given the lexical meaning of *homo* as
*man*, the syntactic rules for the use of the dative and the
singular, and the morphological rules for deriving *homini*
as dative singular, nothing needs to be said about the mean-

ing of *homini* as such. Like literally thousands of such words, it is exhaustively accounted for without having to be referred to specifically. In derivational processes, however, individual statements of meaning, as well as the particularistic listing of forms, are often necessary. For example, the relationship of *hopeful* to *hope* as a paradigmatic model will not apply altogether exactly to the relationship of *careful* to *care,* and still less to that of *artful* to *art.* Hence this, as well as the even more capricious area of compounding, has tended to be treated either incompletely or not at all, and its treatment has been largely left to the dictionary.

In addition to its role as the basic item of dictionary entries and as the reference point for the fundamental grammatical division between morphology and syntax, the lexeme also provided the framework for an exhaustive division of all the words of a language into a limited number of sets, the "parts of speech." These—for example, noun, verb, adjective —had been defined for the Classical languages in terms of morphological and syntactic similarities, which were believed in general to go hand in hand. Thus, in Latin, the adjective could be defined as that class of words (that is, lexemes) that are inflected for number, gender and case as against, for example, nouns, which are inflected only for number and case. But adjectives could also be defined, in terms of their common syntactic function, as modifiers of nouns.

The parts of speech were in practice an identical set that was believed to be valid for all languages and equatable from language to language, because of the essentially identical logical nature of all coherent discourse. The identification of parts of speech in languages that were without the specific morphological and syntactic traits of the Classical languages, which they fitted reasonably well, was necessarily on a translation basis. *Noun* in a language like Burmese was the name for that class of words that were in general translation equivalents of words that belonged to the class of nouns in Latin and Greek and in the modern Western languages. This led naturally to their definition in semantic terms, rather than in terms of morphological characteristic or syntactic function. Thus verbs, nouns, and adjectives might be defined respectively as designating actions, substances, and qualities.

Phonology played a minor role; it consisted essentially of rules of pronunciation for the orthographically given forms. For the ancient languages, which were the focus of interest for comparatists, the primary evidence was in the form of written texts, the pronunciation of which could not be directly known. Moreover, particularly during the earlier period of comparative study, regular comparison could be carried out quite successfully by reference to the letters of the written text rather than by way of the spoken sounds. Grammars of modern languages were, as we have seen, largely normative and the standardization usually took the form of a regularized orthography. Phonology was thus mainly the enunciation of normative pronunciation rules, designed to ensure conformity to the supradialectal standards of the common literary language.

Of the three types of grammars already mentioned— the philological, the literary standard, and the "exotic" non-Western—it was the last that played a seminal role in the development of structuralism during the first half of the twentieth century, because it was in these grammars that the inadequacies of the traditional approach became most clearly apparent. I do not mean to assert that this problem provided the sole occasion for the development of structuralist ideas. Structuralism was a complex movement, which took somewhat different forms in the United States, Great Britain, and the Continent. Moreover, it can be plausibly regarded as only one phase of a much broader movement, which embraces structuralism and functionalism in anthropology and sociology and, in Europe, Gestalt psychology. What is said in this chapter, which is not primarily historical, applies most closely to American linguistic structuralism.

The inadequacies of the dominant nineteenth-century

approach to linguistics did indeed appear most clearly when the field study of non-Western, hitherto unwritten languages began to be undertaken, not only for practical purposes but as an essential part of ethnographic description by the burgeoning science of anthropology. To the ethnographer, trying to describe a hitherto unwritten language, the absence of an indigenous orthography, with a built-in analysis of the sound system, made a systematic phonological approach based on phonetics a prime desideratum. But, as we have seen, phonetics was marginal to the traditional doctrine and no coherent phonological theory existed. In grammar, the scheme of parts of speech and of inflectional categories, which had been developed on the basis of the analysis of a limited range of Western languages, was applicable to languages of very different structure only at the cost of imposing on them categories that were either nonexistent or unimportant, while disregarding others that played a large role in the actual functioning of the language. This suggested that descriptive theory, which was taken for granted during the nineteenth century, when historical interests were in the foreground, needed systematic theoretical attention and that the traditional methodology required drastic overhauling. Moreover, for languages that were without written records and without adequate descriptions, the historical explanations that were derived from the study of earlier texts and from the comparative method that had been applied so successfully in the case of Indo-European and a few other families, were not feasible.

This led to a real revolution in linguistics, the theoretical bases for which were most clearly articulated, although in somewhat different fashion, in the writings of de Saussure on the Continent and in American anthropology and linguistics under the leadership of Franz Boas, Edward Sapir and Leonard Bloomfield.

Theoretical problems of descriptive synchronic linguistics became the center of interest, replacing the nineteenth-century concentration on historical study. Every language, viewed synchronically, was seen as a coherent and unique whole. The purpose of linguistic theory therefore became to provide the methodology and the concepts in terms of which the structure of any language could be discovered and described in its own right, rather than being distorted by the arbitrary imposition of Western habits of hearing or of grammatical categorizing.

Although the methods by which these ends were to be attained were themselves subject to constant change and development, and differed considerably, to begin with, in Europe and the United States, nevertheless something like a uniform model ultimately developed, or perhaps one should rather speak of a series of methods which, in spite of great surface variation, showed an underlying unity. The tendencies of this era may be most consistently summed up in a model that has been called "item-and-arrangement." This model is susceptible of reasonably clear and coherent statement, although that inevitably transforms it into a kind of caricature, not like the practice of any particular linguist, and in fact a perfect straw man for the next group of revolutionaries when they seek to explain what they are rebelling against. (These same observations apply, incidentally, *mutatis mutandis* to the description of traditional nineteenth-century grammatical theory by the structuralists during the course of *their* revolt.) In what follows, I shall discuss structuralism in certain of its general aspects which are more or less common to all schools and approaches, but with particular reference to the American variety and to what may be considered its most characteristic form, that of item-and-arrangement.

The marginal position of phonology in the traditional approach was noted earlier. In structuralism, this was reversed. The theoretical treatment of phonological problems became the central problem in the most influential of the European structuralist approaches, that of the Prague School; this also held true for England and the United States. Structuralism had arisen within the context of phonological theory; only later did it attack grammatical problems in serious fashion and then largely through the use of concepts that had been developed during the earlier period of concentration on phonology.

The choice of an approach through phonology rather than from the other end, as it were, through syntax, was more than a merely technical decision. It meant that the analyst was in the position of the hearer. Indeed, especially in the United States, linguistic theory became the statement of procedures for an idealized field worker who was encountering an exotic language for the first time, and for whom primary evidence was the utterances of his informant. The approach was therefore highly empirical; in fact, it was in fundamental agreement with the prevailing psychological theory of behaviorism. By contrast with traditional grammar, it was essentially nonnormative. The evidence for language was the reality of what people actually said, rather than normative judgments about that reality. There was likewise a tendency to discount as evidence informant reactions and judgments about their own speech, since these involved introspective processes that went under the name of mentalism and were not susceptible of investigation.

This also affected the attitude toward semantics. In fact, utterances in a strange tongue were elicited primarily as translation equivalences, and grammatical analysis took the form of the analysis of texts that had been subjected to semantic interpretation. It was felt by many, however, that translation and semantic interpretation once again involved complex and unobservable mental data. Ideally, it should be possible to carry through a phonological and grammatical analysis of a language, on the basis of the empirically given evidence of the informant's utterance, without having to resort to meaning. It was sometimes maintained that the procedures for doing this were actually available and that the resort to meaning was merely a theoretically nonessential shortcut, a heuristic device, as it were. The tendency to exclude semantics from linguistics was not motivated solely by the theoretical rejection of mentalism, but had complex roots, among which was the desire to delimit an autonomous area for linguistics. This meant for some the notion that since *designation*, the central concept of lexicographical semantics, constituted a relation between a linguistic and a nonlinguistic item—for example, between the word *table* and the object that the word designates, it was an "impure" notion that had no place in linguistics. Another factor in this position was that rejection of the traditional method of defining parts of speech for "exotic" languages by semantic equivalence with the categories of the Classical languages was one aspect of a general doubt about the feasibility of including semantic procedures at all in a scientific linguistics.

The basic problem for phonological theory in this context was to devise analytic procedures that, starting with perceived sounds, would arrive at the phonological units that are peculiar to each linguistic structure. Such a result would not distort the sound system of the language under investigation through perceptual and classificatory biases arising from the observer's own linguistic habits. In principle, then, every qualified linguist, whatever his own primary linguistic background, would arrive at the same system for any particular language. The system thus arrived at would be, in some sense, the "real" system of the language; it would do justice to the language's uniqueness, its individuality and its organizing principles, which might be, in some cases, very different from those that the linguist had encountered in the languages of the ancient world and of modern Europe that were more familiar to him. The universal elements were the panhuman categories of phonetics —the *etic* framework, as it later came to be called—and the analytic procedures of phonological theory. It was these that made phonology a teachable science with replicable results. The results for each language were, however unique, the *emic* elements and their arrangement, which reflected the true structure of the language.[2]

The extent of the success with which this goal of phonology was attained, as well as the manner in which it was attained, are discussed in some detail in the next chapter. For the present, it is sufficient to note that the solution was expressed in terms of minimal units, called *phonemes*. In the prevailing American analysis, before European influence had exerted its effect, the phonemes, like the atoms of classical chemical theory, were not further analyzable. Relatively small in number, by their combinations in sequences they made up all the meaningful sequences of the language. Among the Prague theorists, the phonemes were not regarded as ultimate, each being a combination of a number of features; the features for any language were, in this theory, fewer in number than the phonemes. In either case, the phonological structure was based on a set of irreducible fundamental units, from combinations of which were constructed the sentences of a language.

In its American version, the description of the phonological system of a language had three aspects. The first was identification of the fundamental units, the phonemes. The second was establishment of the set of rules by which each of these units showed variant phonetic forms (*allophones*) in relation to surrounding phonemes—that is, in terms of what was called its "environment." (This environment had itself to be specified in purely phonetic terms.) Finally, there were rules of permitted sequences of the phonemic elements. Thus phonology was a self-contained system, describable without reference to the grammatical structures of the language, although the functioning units on the grammatical level were made up of elements from the more fundamental level.

The treatment of grammar involved at one and the same time a virtually complete methodological parallelism with the phonological level and substantive separation from that level under the doctrine of distinctness of levels. This doctrine has already been illustrated for phonology in the canon that only phonological environments can be referred to in a statement of the rules for allophonic variation.

For such a parallel treatment of grammar and phonology, the first requirement was the isolation of a minimal functional unit that would be the elementary building block corresponding to the phoneme. The word, the basic unit of traditional grammar, was clearly unsuited for this role, since it often exhibited a complex internal structure. For example, the English word *hats* seemed to be divisible into two parts (*hat-s*), *leaders* into three *lead-er-s*), and *unhesitatingly* into at least four (*un-hesitat-ing-ly*).

Such units, which were in general smaller than words and not further divisible into meaningful parts, were called *morphemes*. They were obviously, however, far more numerous than the phonemes, and ran into the thousands for any natural language. As the basic grammatical units of the new approach, they were also to take over the traditional function of words as the unit of dictionary entries. The lexicon was therefore to be a list of the morphemes of the language, along with their meanings. One consequence of this approach was that the old distinction between lexical word meaning and the meaning of grammatical categories which formed part of the grammar lost its theoretical significance. Presumably, for English there would be an entry in the morpheme list for *carry* and another for *-d* (past), without there being any truly significant difference in the nature of the meaning involved. Such morpheme dictionaries were compiled for certain "exotic" languages, particularly Amerindian, but this approach to dictionary making never exercised any significant influence on lexicographical practice in regard to the major literary languages.

Like the phoneme, the morpheme had its variants; they were called *allomorphs* as a terminological parallel to the allophones of phonology. Allophones of the same phoneme were phonetically different forms of the same fundamental unit. The difference between allophones was assumed to be nonfunctional, in that they did not contrast with one another. This could be deduced from the rules of distribution—that is, rules that assigned each variant to a different set among mutually exclusive environments. In the same way, certain morphemes occurred in variant forms, the allomorphs, which were sequences that differed in their phonemic composition. Rules could be stated in terms of surrounding morphemes, so that each morpheme could be assigned to one particular set among mutually exclusive environments.

An example is the noun plural morpheme in English. It takes such differing phonemic forms as /s/, for example, /hæt-s/ *hats;* /z/, for example, /hænd-z/ *hands;* /ɪz/, for example, /dɪšɪz/ *dishes;* /n̩/, for example, /aks-n̩/ *oxen,* and so forth. Each of these forms can be assigned to a set of environments. Sometimes, as with /s/, which occurs when the noun plural is preceded by any morpheme that ends in a voiceless phoneme, there is a common phonological feature for the entire set. Such allomorphs are therefore said to be phonologically conditioned. For such an allomorph as /n̩/, however, the only environment is the specific morpheme {aks} *ox.*[3] Where a specific list of one or more morphemes is involved, the conditioning is said to be grammatical or morphological, since it requires reference to specific morphemes.

The aspect of grammar that had to do with the variant phonemic shapes of the allomorphs of the morphemes was called *morphophonemics.* The postulates of a system of morphophonemics that conformed to the "item-and-arrangement" ideal would then be as follows. Every allomorph would consist of some overt sequence of phonemes, and every phoneme would be assigned to one and only one allomorph. Thus, in /aks-n̩/, the first three phonemes were assigned to the (only) allomorph of {aks}, and the last two to one of the numerous variant allomorphs of the plural form (sometimes symbolized by $\{Z_1\}$). A second postulate would be that every allomorph would be assignable unambiguously to some morpheme; this would include the frequent case in which an allomorph was the only member of a morpheme that appeared everywhere in the same phonemic shape. Further, each of the variant allomorphs of the same morpheme would have to be assigned to a specific set of environments that did not overlap with that of any other allomorph of the same morpheme. It was a corollary of this approach that there is no priority among the various allomorphs of the same morpheme, and that each must have an overt shape, consisting of a sequence of phonemes, although not necessarily a continuous sequence. Similarly, there is no hierarchy among the morphemes in a word as between stem and inflection affix; they simply coexist.

Sentences are sequences of morphemes, the minimal units of grammatical structure. Hence the remainder of grammar, sentence formation, is to be encompassed by rules about the possible combinations of morphemes that are analogous to the rules for permitted sequences of phonemes in phonology. The far greater complexity of grammar, however, had raised certain problems that are not encountered in phonology. Two particular aspects of this complexity may be singled out for attention: One has to do with the vastly greater number of individual units involved, since morphemes are to be reckoned in the thousands; the other is the evident internal complexity of the sentence, as it is mirrored in the hierarchy of traditional grammatical terminology of word, phrase, clause, and sentence.

In regard to the first of these aspects, the solution was evidently to deal not with morphemes, but with classes of morphemes—that is, with sets whose members behaved similarly or identically. Since the criterion of similarity in this context ought not to be meaning, it was to be, once again, the basic concept of both morphophonemic and phonological theory—namely, distribution. A morpheme class was, ideally, a set of morphemes that occurred in the same environments, so that they were equivalent for all combinatory statements. If this were so, then sentence-formation rules could be exclusively in terms of such classes, rather than by individual morphemes, a procedure that would be intolerably complicated.

Here, once again, the contrast with traditional grammar

is striking. The morpheme classes correspond to the "parts of speech" in traditional grammar, in that they are the relatively small set of basic classes to which all meaningful elements are assigned and in terms of which sentence structure is specified. Unlike the parts of speech, however, they are not presumed to be a fixed set with constant semantic properties and therefore found in all languages. Rather, just as universal procedures of a distributional sort make possible the discovery of the true phonological system of each language, without the burden of preconceptions that arise as the result of the uncritical imposition of the observer's own background, so too in grammar it should be possible by objective distributional methods to discover the functionally relevant morpheme classes of the language. In order to avoid misconceptions, it might even be better to use arbitrary symbols instead of traditional grammatical labels. Thus Fries heroically introduced terms such as "Class 1" instead of the "noun" of traditional English grammar.[4]

The other great problem, that of the hierarchy within the sentence, was once again attacked by distributional methods. A relevant subpart of a sentence, such as a phrase, could be recognized as a unit because it occurred in the same environments as some smaller unit. For example, in the sentence *I saw him in the house*, the phrase *in the house* was a functioning unit because there were smaller units, such as the adverb *there*, that occurred in the same environments. Thus, the structure of complex sentences might be described by repeated substitutions of longer and longer strings of morphemes for shorter ones.[5] In this procedure, as contrasted with that of the traditional approach, the word was dethroned from its fundamental position as the dividing line between morphology and syntax. At best, it was one among a number of possible levels from the morpheme to the sentence, but with no special status in this regard. Since the grammatical structure of each language has to be discovered by objective procedures without any a priori assumptions, it might be expected that a number of types of such hierarchies would occur in the world's languages and that some would not possess a unit that was reasonably equatable with the word.

Any subpart of a sentence that comes to be a grammatically functioning part of the whole, as the result of such substitution techniques, may be called a *constituent*. Thus, in the sentence *I saw the footrails in the bar*, *in the bar* is a constituent, as are, at a lower level, *bar*, *footrail*, and at a still lower level, *foot-*, *-rail*, and *-s*. On the other hand, *-rails in* is not a constituent nor is *I saw the*. From the top down, as it were, one could divide the sentence into its major constituents, each of these in turn into lower-level constituents, and so on, down to the morpheme. Such a sentence analysis resembled that of the traditional sentence parsing by diagram, which first divided a complex sentence into a main and subordinate clause, each of these in turn into subject and predicate, and so on. The structural approach to grammar was designed to provide a method for parsing any given sentence of a language by *immediate constituent* (IC) *analysis*, as this procedure was called. The particular divisions would be justified, chiefly in accordance with the general trend of the whole approach, as being parts for which shorter sequences of simpler internal structure could be substituted.

The underlying themes of the structuralist approach of the type just outlined may be summarized as follows. The utterances of a language constitute a set of sequences of discrete items. They may be analyzed as consisting of atom-like minimal units on two levels, the phonological and the grammatical. The minimal unit of the grammatical level, the morpheme, generally consists of sequences of the unit of the phonological level, the phoneme; otherwise, they are independent and can be investigated by themselves. On each level, the task of description is to distinguish the fundamental units, their variants in environments that are statable in terms of that level, and their rules of combination. They are discovered precisely by their "privileges of occurrence"

—that is, distributionally. Thus, a morpheme class is a set of morphemes that occur in the same environment and are therefore substitutable for each other. By such procedures, it is possible, without taking meaning into consideration, to discover the functional elements of each language. In the lexicon, each morpheme, as the minimal meaningful unit, was to be listed together with its meaning.

The attempt to found a scientific descriptive linguistics along these lines can now be seen to have failed in every major respect. The fact that phonology cannot be dealt with adequately in isolation from grammar is shown in some detail in the following chapter. In grammar, for example, it proved impossible to define the morpheme in a non-arbitrary fashion and in conformity with the intuition and the practice of linguists. Given the existence of allomorphs, the morphophonemics of a language could not be stated by strictly item-and-arrangement procedures, in which each allomorph consisted of phonemes. For example, given that there is a past morpheme in English with a very common allomorph -*d* (e.g., in *carrie-d*), there must be a different allomorph of the same morpheme in *took* /tuk/. But the contrast with *take* suggested that the allomorph of the past was -*oo*- /u/. This, however, would lead to the conclusion that the morpheme meaning *to take* is the remainder, the discontinuous /t-k/. In that case economy demands that it also be /t-k/ in the present. Given that, there is a morpheme of the present with an allomorph -*a-e* /ej/ in *take*. We are therefore forced to admit the existence of a present morpheme. But if there is one, it must surely occur in the present form *carry*, where it does not take overt form. The result was to postulate a zero in these latter cases, with the proviso that it should never be the sole allomorph.

An alternative solution for analyzing *took* abandoned the basic postulates described above, and spoke instead of a *process*, rather than an arrangement. The past allomorph of *take* was a replacive, *ej* ← *u*, which consisted of a replacement of *u* by *ej*. If we follow this out consistently, *carried* would also be obtained by starting with the present *carry* and adding *-d*. This approach was thus called *item-and-process*. It was clearly much more like traditional grammar, in which the base had priority over the inflection, and the inflection was said to be added (suffixed, prefixed, etc.). In certain cases, a much neater statement was obviously obtainable by the even more drastic process of deletion (*subtractives*).[6]

But the most acute problems had to do with syntax. The fundamental operation of substitution, in order to determine whether two morphemes had, in fact, the same distribution and therefore belonged to the same class, could not be carried out in the same relatively simple fashion as it is in phonology, where the number of sounds and their classes of possible environments are both strictly limited. For example, we would certainly conjecture that *man* and *boy* should belong to the same morpheme class. Given the great variety of sentences, however, that will appear in spontaneous text, the chance of finding even a few pairs of sentences in which *man* and *boy* directly contrast—for example, (1) *The man came*, (2) *The boy came*—will probably be small. But more is required than just a few occurrences of this type. In order to establish identity of distribution, there must be for every sentence in the corpus that contains *boy* a corresponding one that differs only in the fact that it has *man* in place of *boy*; similarly, for every sentence that contains *boy*, there must be one that has *man* in its place.

There are two ways out, both of them destructive of the basic assumptions of the type of structuralism being considered here. One is to make up the corresponding sentences that have not occurred in the actual text, but for that we must have some criterion of acceptability. Presumably, we would ask the informant, but this runs counter to the principle of not appealing to the informant's intuitions about his language. Besides, in practice, questions of this sort will receive varying responses. The other alternative is for the linguist to judge whether the missing sentences are possible; but this would mean that he was dealing with a universe of "possible sentences," which extended beyond those empirically given in the corpus. This is, of course, one consequence of the fact referred to earlier, that the sentences of a language are an infinite set.

The development of immediate constitutent analysis brought into sharp relief the inability of distributional theory to deal with syntax. Where was the supposed rigor of scientific linguistics, in contrast to the traditional grammar, when it turned out that IC analysis was virtually identical with the familiar parsing diagrams of school grammars? It was clear that this kind of sentence analysis was arrived at by reference to semantic intuition and could be justified, if at all, only by subsequent distributional procedures, which could not in fact be carried out without reference to a non-empirical infinity of possible sentences.

The revolution that has been produced in American linguistics by the rise of transformational grammar is an attempt to escape from these dilemmas by a virtually complete reversal of basic approach. Just as structuralism started as a phonological theory because traditional linguistics was weakest in that area, so transformational grammar began with syntax, a weak sector in all earlier linguistic theory and the last and least successfully treated by the structuralists. In so doing, it naturally rejected the empirical approach that was concordant with American psychological behaviorism, which had characterized the linguistics of the previous period. Linguistics need not limit itself to the analysis of the empirically given in terms of constructs that are merely classes and combinations of actually occurring elements. In morphophonemics, for example, basic forms are set up for morphemes that need not coincide with any actually occurring form. This device had already been used in the previous period by some linguists who inclined toward the item-and-process approach, an approach that was largely incorporated into the new theory. The emphasis is not on the products themselves, as being the first data encountered empirically, but rather on the rules that could produce them. These rules are partially ordered: Certain ones must be applied before others, or unacceptable combinations will be produced. Hence, the metaphor of movement, of diachrony, as it were, is incorporated within synchrony. It is this mechanism of a finite set of ordered rules that is capable of producing an infinity of sentences that is the object of the linguist's study. For any particular language, the purpose of his theoretic endeavor is to construct this mechanism, for which the data of performance provide evidence. The approach is therefore called *generative*.

A further important point of difference from the structuralist period is the renewal of attention to the universal aspects of language, in place of the structuralist emphasis on each language as possessing a unique structure. Each language is, of course, unique; but making the overall goal simply that of specifying each unique structure, without at the same time seeking for the common basis that is present in all languages, destroys the possibility of generalization, which is the presumed aim of scientific endeavor.

In these and other respects, generative transformational theory is closer to earlier traditional linguistics than it is to structuralism. At the same time, structuralism made enormous technical contributions in linguistic analysis, which are acknowledged in principle and, to a great extent, utilized.[7] Nevertheless, this transformational grammar is not simply a more rigorous statement of the older traditional linguistics. It has certain novel and highly ambitious goals, one of which is the ideal of explicitness. The grammar of a language should contain rules that are capable of generating all the grammatical sentences of the language, without producing any that are ungrammatical. All the aspects of grammar that were traditionally treated separately—phonology, semantics, and syntax—are contained in an overall structure of rules of specified forms. Perhaps most characteristically, all generalizations about the language are to be stated within the grammar, by choosing among alternatives on a "principled basis"—that is, a basis that can be justified by some overall consideration of scientific method.

It is admitted that as yet no single language—even English, which has been most completely analyzed—has as yet been adequately described in accordance with these standards. The theory is of interest and value in that, for the first time in the history of linguistics, it takes account of the full seriousness of the notion of explanation within the framework of descriptive synchronic linguistics. In order to carry this out fully, if indeed it can be done at all, there will very likely have to be further changes, and far from trivial ones, in the theory; until now, however, it has shown a remarkable ability to overcome difficulties by fundamental reformulations. The remaining parts of this work are a tacit denial, however, that any theory of this kind can be *the* theory of language in the sense that it will contain all kinds of explanations that are theoretically relevant—for example, to mention but a few, explanations that are concerned with language change, the relation of the human articulatory and perceptual apparatus to the general features of phonological systems, the cultural conditions of semantic change, and the sociopolitical conditions for dialect and language differentiation. In order to encompass these other factors, a less restrictive notion of explanation is required.

In the following chapter, we trace, within the more restricted domain of phonology, the general development of linguistic theory just described. This treatment has the supplementary purpose of providing some factual background for the later discussion of synchronic and diachronic generalizations, the material for which is largely drawn from phonology.

# V

# PHONOLOGY

The sounds of speech seem to function in an ordered sequence of discrete elements, composed of a relatively small number of distinct sound types. Alphabetic writing, with its limited set of symbols, is an approximate representation of such ordered chains of sounds. The degree of correspondence between sound and symbol depends on the orthographic system employed. The popular view is that, in a truly rational alphabet, there would be a one-to-one relation between sound and orthographic symbol: every distinct sound would be represented by only one written symbol, and every symbol would stand for only one sound. As we shall see, it did not prove to be possible, in the period preceding the development of modern structural linguistics, to found a scientific phonology by using as the basic units distinguishable sounds of the sort that would be represented unambiguously in such an ideal orthography; furthermore, this approach is not in accordance with the analysis that is implicit in traditional alphabetic writing. Structural linguistics developed instead the concept of the phoneme, a phonological unit that was not based on mere physical distinguishability, but rather reflected only those differences in sound that have a functional role in the overall linguistic system. We shall also see how, in spite of the very real merits that have until now made the phoneme, in one form or another, the basic unit of most phonological analysis, it has in its turn run into basic difficulties, whose solution requires an approach that at least in some respects calls for theoretical innovations.

Although phonetic science had a significant history prior to the nineteenth century, it was during that century that developments in it took place of relevance to our present discussion. Most importantly, during this period there came into being an overall system, based chiefly on articulatory characteristics, in terms of which any sound that occurred in any language could be defined by reference to a limited, in fact a quite small, number of parameters. Thus, for consonants, it was sufficient to refer to one or more places in the speech tract above the glottis in which there was a constriction, together with the type of constriction, and the nature of the accompanying glottal adjustment. In order to define the initial sound of the English word *boy*, for example, one had to specify the point of articulation (here *bilabial*, since both lips are involved), the type of constriction (*complete closure*), and the accompanying vibration of the vocal cords (*voice*). Such a description could be abbreviated in terms of a fairly standardized terminology, so that the initial sound of *boy* could be called a *bilabial voiced stop*, an expression in which the point of articulation, glottal activity, and type of closure are successively stated.

Where two supraglottal points of constriction were involved, one of them, usually the greater constriction, was made primary in the terminology and the other treated as a modification. Thus the [b] with its closure of the lips might under some circumstances be accompanied by a simultaneous approximation of the front of the tongue to the hard palate, which by itself would produce a [y]. This second articulation was called *palatalization* and the total articulation was called a *bilabial voiced palatalized stop.* The vowels were classified according to three basic coordinates, which differed from those of the consonants: height of the tongue, placement of the highest part of the tongue on a front-back dimension, and lip rounding. For example, the vowel of the English word *beat* would be described, for some speakers at least, as *high, front,* and *unrounded.* Here too, other aspects of the articulation were treated as secondary modifications. For example, if the velic, the back of the soft palate, was lowered so that air also escaped from the nose, the vowel was said to be nasalized.

Each sound was thus defined, as it were statically, by a set of positions of the vocal organs. It was recognized that there were inevitably movements from one position to another, called *glides,* but these were believed to be determined by the initial and terminal positions and in any case to be swift and generally inaudible. For one class of sounds, *diphthongs,* in which the sound consisted wholly in the movement from one vowel position to another, it was recognized that the glide was the essential component. Difficulties of another sort were raised by such features as duration and stress; unlike the features described earlier, these could not be defined in isolation but only in relation to other occurrences in the speech continuum. A long vowel in rapid speech might actually be of shorter duration than a short vowel in more deliberate speech. Similarly, a vowel is classified as stressed by virtue of the fact that it exceeds the surrounding vowels in prominence, not in terms of an absolute quality, independent of the vowel's location.

The system of phonetic analysis, as it developed, was thus fundamentally based on the notion of a succession of sounds, each defined statically in terms of a finite though rather loosely defined set of coordinates, with a residue of other relational and transitional concepts.

Along with this analysis, students of phonetics developed, as part of their training, skill in recognizing and recording the successions of sounds of a language. The methods of phonetics were not only applied to the relatively well-known standard languages but were also utilized for dialect-atlas work and for the study of hitherto unwritten languages.

The common method of transcription was that of the International Phonetic Association, or some variant of it.[1] The principle of this transcription was that every distinguishable sound should be represented by a distinct symbol, and the Latin alphabet was therefore extended by the invention of many new symbols. The attempt to represent each distinct sound by a distinct symbol was, however, obviously impractical, and the analysis of sounds by means of the coordinates mentioned earlier was therefore incorporated to some degree into the phonetic alphabet. For example, instead of each nasalized vowel being symbolized by an independent and similarly unanalyzable symbol, such a "secondary feature" as nasalization was indicated by a tilde ($\sim$) over the symbol for the corresponding nonnasalized vowel.

To the phoneticians of the latter part of the nineteenth and the early twentieth century, the application of such methods of phonetic analysis and its accompanying transcription constituted an obvious scientific advance. Every possible speech sound was provided for in the system, so that the worker who had been trained in it could produce an accurate and hence scientifically valid record. From the practical point of view, the problem of devising a truly phonetic and hence correct alphabetic orthography for each language of the world seemed in principle to have been solved. All that was necessary was to record all the sounds of the language accurately in the International Phonetic Alphabet, or in some variation of it, and the ideal of a one-to-one correspondence between symbol and sound would be attained. Only human inertia and vested interests stood in the way of a perfect orthography for the standard languages.

Nevertheless, a number of serious difficulties were becoming evident. The growth of instrumental phonetics during the last decades of the nineteenth century showed that, if one truly wanted accuracy, even the best-trained phonetician could not produce adequate analyses. Sounds that seemed the same to the phonetician were shown to differ when they were examined by the methods of the phonetics laboratory. In fact, it became apparent that even the "same word," pronounced by the same speaker on different occasions, was always physically different on each separate occasion.

Although these facts could be and later were used by the structuralist opponents of a purely phonetic approach, there were other even more immediate difficulties, for which the remedy could not be greater accuracy of transcription, even when the difficulties were limited to differences perceivable without instrumentation.

It is true that scientific phonetics was an advance over the previous naïve transcriptions by untrained workers, who simply wrote down what they heard in terms of the sound distinctions of their own languages. Such methods had naturally produced a biased record. The sound systems of all languages, as recorded by untrained English-speaking observers, tended to look roughly alike, while the same language, recorded by an untrained English transcriber and an untrained French one, came out differently. This bias was overcome—in principle at least—by the newer methods of scientific phonetics. Any phonetician, regardless of his own first language, should be able by these methods to produce the same objectively verifiable analysis of the sounds of a given language.

But this was accomplished at a price. The phoneticians were producing more and more detailed records that somehow seemed to run counter to the reactions of speakers of the language as to what was linguistically relevant and, indeed, counter to the intuitions that underlay alphabetical writing itself.

For example, phoneticians noted that what the ordinary

speaker of English considered to be the same *k* sound had phonetically distinguishable forms, which had to be recorded differently in an accurate phonetic transcription. Thus the *k* in the word *kin* had an audible puff of breath following it, called *aspiration,* and so would be transcribed phonetically as [kᶜ], while the *k* of *skill,* having no such aspiration, would be symbolized by [k]. The final sound in the word *pack* did not have an audible release of any sort and so should be written [k⁼], and so on.

There were, then, sound differences, easily and reliably recognized by a trained phonetician, that were ordinarily disregarded or not even heard by speakers of the language and whose difference somehow seemed irrelevant to them. On the other hand, there were other differences that were regularly recorded in the orthography and did seem important to the speakers—for example, the difference between any phonetic variation of *k* and any phonetic variation of *t.* The answer could not be simply that certain sound differences, being physically smaller, just did not matter. Two of the forms of the English *k* mentioned earlier, the aspirated and the unaspirated, were felt by speakers of other languages—for example, Hindi—to be significantly different and were therefore differentiated in their orthography.

In order to discover that the relations between [kᶜ] and [k] were different in English and Hindi, in spite of the practical phonetic identity of the sounds in the two languages, one did not have to rely on the judgments of the speakers of the language. The most easily observable phenomenon that underlay this difference in psychological response was the following: Where, as in Hindi, [k] and [kᶜ] were viewed by speakers as separate sounds, they served to distinguish meanings; where, as in English, they were viewed by speakers as being the same, they did not distinguish meanings. The simplest demonstration that this was so was to note that there were instances in Hindi of so-called minimal pairs— that is, everything else being constant, two forms with different meanings were distinguished phonetically solely by the difference in question. Thus, in Hindi, [kʰiˑl] means *parched grain* and [kiˑl] means *nail*. In English, no example of this could be found.

Evidently, then, there were two levels of analysis. One was the phonetic level of the actual sounds. In this regard, while languages might agree in their possession of certain sounds, they could differ in their functional utilization of these same sounds. Where physically different sounds did not serve to distinguish forms with different meanings, they might be considered members of the same unit on a higher level. This level was called the *phonemic level,* and such units were called *phonemes.* Thus, in both Hindi and English, the sounds [k] and [kʰ] existed on the phonetic level; in English, however, there was a single phoneme /k/, to which all occurrences of [k], [kʰ], [k⁼] and still others were assigned, whereas in Hindi there were two separate phonemes /k/ and /kʰ/.

The theory of two levels of analysis, a lower physical level and a higher functional level, rapidly gained ground during the 1920's and 1930's, and became the foundation of the new structural linguistics. Besides furnishing a way out of the impasse described earlier, it fitted in well with the currently developing structural-functional trends in anthropology and in Gestalt psychology. At this stage, it seemed natural to consider the phoneme both functionally, as a unit that differentiated meanings, and mentalistically, as a psychological unit. To speakers of English, in spite of obvious phonetic differences, the phoneme /k/, for example, seemed to function in consciousness as a unitary element and to possess psychological reality.

In American linguistics, however, the concept of the phoneme as a psychological unit with the function of semantic differentiation ceased, with the rise of behaviorism, to conform to the prevalent intellectual currents. Psychological units smacked of mentalism and semantics clearly involved the functioning of higher mental processes. From this point of view, it would be far more satisfactory, while maintaining the distinction between phonetic and phonemic levels, to define the phoneme by the logical manipulation of observables—namely, sounds—without recourse to meaning or to the psychological responses of the speaker.

There were indeed difficulties in the approach indicated above. Put most simply, two sounds were taken to belong to the same phoneme if at least one minimal pair could be produced and not to belong to the same phoneme if a pair of that sort could not be produced. But there are instances in which, particularly if the sounds are relatively infrequent and occur in different positions in the syllable, it is difficult, even impossible, to find a minimal contrast. Yet the same speaker's intuition, on which we relied to tell us that there is no phonemic difference between [kʻ] and [k], tells us just as surely that the English sound [ž] as in *azure*, is phonemically distinct from the final [ŋ] of *sing*, even though no minimal pair can be produced. Further, how can we tell at what point to give up our search for minimal pairs?

The distributional approach that developed in the United States, chiefly during the 1940's and 1950's, seemed to be at once objective and rigorous, in that it involved no appeal to meaning differences, and to offer a solution to the problems that had been raised by reliance on the semantic differentiating function.

Let us consider once more the example of the variant forms of the English /k/ phoneme. If we were to make a list of those cases in which the unaspirated variant [k] occurs, we would find that, from the phonetic point of view, they are not random. In every instance, the [k] is preceded by [s] in the same syllable and followed by a vowel—for example, *skin, ski, scare, scold,* and so on. In examples with strong aspiration, we find that an [s] does not precede in the same syllable and that the following vowel is stressed—for example, *can, cold, caper.* Similarly, all the other variants of the /k/ phoneme are found to occur only under certain conditions that are specifiable in terms of neighboring sounds. We may generalize this procedure in terms of the following concepts. Let us call the remainder of the sequence in which any sound occurs its environment: Thus, in *skin* [skin], the environment of [k] is [s-in]. The rule just mentioned regarding the occurrence of [k] may then be stated in terms of the common characteristics of all such environments. The variant [k] occurs only in environments of the type [s-V . . .], where V stands for any vowel. When our rule for the aspirated form [kᶜ] is likewise stated in terms of environments, we can see that it excludes instances of [s-V . . .], and that the environments of [kᶜ] and [k] are therefore mutually exclusive. When the total sets of environments (called the *distribution*) of two sounds are mutually exclusive, they cannot contrast. Minimal contrast, as in Hindi [kiil] versus [kᶜiil], is based on occurrence in at least one identical environment (in this instance [-iil]).

It is evident that, if we can characterize the distribution of each of a set of variant sounds by simple rules of this kind, which involve the mutual exclusiveness of their environments, it will follow that, short of a violation of the rules we have set up, no contrast can occur. We now have reason for our confidence that no example of minimal contrast will be found for English [kᶜ] and [k]. On the other hand, for [ž] and [ŋ], even if we have not found an actual minimal pair, no reasonably simple rule can be discovered that will tell us, for any environment, which of the two should be expected, and we are therefore entitled to conclude that the absence of an example is essentially accidental, and due primarily to the statistical infrequency of the two sounds. We would not be surprised, then, if an example were to be found, since it would not be a violation of any rule that had already been set up.

The same concept of *distribution* as the totality of environments can be employed in dealing with another situation that arises, although not so commonly as that of complementary distribution. Sometimes it is found that two distinguishably different sounds may occur in variant forms of the same word, without any apparent difference in meaning.

Thus, in the word *put,* the final *t* may be either unreleased [t⁼] or released with aspiration [tᶜ]. Most commonly, as in this example, the variation is confined to a single class of environments (*word final*), but this is not necessary. If the example is not an isolated one—in this case, it is not—it may be possible to establish a rule of the following type. Whenever in word final a form in final [t⁼] is found, there is always a corresponding one with [tᶜ] and vice versa. This situation, known as *free variation,* can also be described in terms of environment, in this case identity, since [t⁼] and [tᶜ] can always substitute for each other, at least in the restricted set of word-final environments.

If we use Venn circles to indicate the classes of environments, we can see that the three logically possible cases are accounted for. If *a* and *b* represent the distributions of two different sounds, then, in the diagram below, Case 1 is that of complementary distribution (mutually exclusive distribution), Case 2 that of free variation (identical distribution), and Case 3 that of contrast, only part of the distribution in common (minimal pairs).

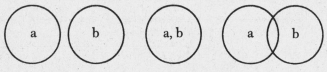

Case 1          Case 2          Case 3

Figure 1

We have thus apparently succeeded in defining the phoneme as consisting of member sounds (allophones) with certain distributional relations. Wherever two sounds are either in complementary distribution, based on simply statable rules, or in free variation, they belong to the same phoneme; wherever they are not, they belong to different phonemes. In this distributional approach, not only is there no overt appeal to meaning, since the distribution is in terms of the neighboring sounds only, but even the specific nature of the sounds is irrelevant. For example, if all the sounds were to receive numerical designations, then the rule regarding the complementary distribution of [k] and [kᶜ] would still be statable—for example, phones (physically distinguishable sound types) 17 and 18 have mutually exclusive distributions, because every environment of 17 [k] has 4 [s] immediately preceding, while this is never true of 18 [kᶜ]. It is evident that all we need to know about the sounds is whether they are the same or different. This aspect of the procedure can be characterized as *abstraction from phonic content*.

For all its seeming attractiveness, however, the purely distributional approach just outlined can be shown to be inadequate. A procedural definition may be shown to be defective either because of some purely logical internal inconsistency or because, when the procedure is carried out, it produces results that are clearly not in concordance with the concept as it was understood before definition—that is, what is being defined is no longer what we set out to define in the first place. In the present instance, it can be shown that the definition fails on both scores, both on consistency and on validity. Consider the statement that two phones are members of the same phoneme if they are in complementary distribution. In Case 1 of Figure 1, this means that the distribution of phones will be mutually exclusive. But if $a$ and $b$ belong to the same phoneme, and if $b$ is in complementary distribution with some third phone $c$, then by the same definition $b$ and $c$ belong to the same phoneme. It is, of course, an elementary logical requirement that membership in the same class be transitive; that is, if $a$ and $b$ belong to the same class, and $b$ and $c$ belong to the same class, then $a$ and $c$ must likewise belong to the same class.[2] It is not difficult, however, to construct a diagram (see, for example, Figure 2), in which this transitivity will not hold—that is, *a*

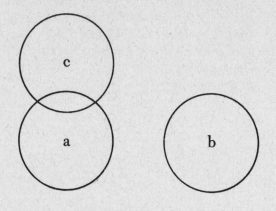

Figure 2

will be in complementary distribution with *b*, and *b* with *c*, but *a* will still not be in complementary distribution with *c*. These two phones will, therefore, represent Case 3 of Figure 1—that is, they will belong to different phonemes.

Actual examples can be cited that exemplify this dilemma. The rule in English according to which unaspirated *k* [k] occurs after [s] when it is before a vowel, while aspirated *k* [kᶜ] does not occur in this class of environments, is exactly paralleled by the distribution of the other unvoiced stops in English, /p/ and /t/. Thus [k], [p], and [t] are all equally in complementary distribution with the corresponding aspirated consonants [kᶜ], [pᶜ], and [tᶜ]. We could therefore assert, as before, that [k] belongs to the same phoneme as [kᶜ] because it is in complementary distribution with it, but we could as well state that [k] must belong to the same phoneme as [pᶜ] because [k] and [pᶜ] are also in complementary distribution. Hence [pᶜ] and [kᶜ] should belong to the same phoneme, but nevertheless, since they are in fact obviously in contrast, they should belong to different phonemes.

The frequently discussed case of [h] and [ŋ] in English demonstrates that, even where complementary distribution does not involve logical difficulties, it may on occasion lead to results that lack validity, in that they do not conform to presystematic notions of what is meant by the phoneme as a functioning unit in the sound system of a language. Since *h* occurs only in syllable initial position and [ŋ] (the sound of *-ng* in *hang*) only in syllable final, they are in complementary distribution. Yet, to regard them as variants of the same phonemic unit runs counter to the intuitions of both speakers and linguists and, in fact, that conclusion has been avoided. In the light of both these examples, it is evident that one cannot abstract from phonic substance. In American phonemic theory, this problem was dealt with in most instances by adding the requirement of phonetic similarity to the distributional criteria. Two phones could then be regarded as members of the same phoneme if they were either in complementary distribution or in free variation *and* if they were phonetically similar. Thus [h] and [ŋ] were considered too dissimilar to be members of the same phoneme, while [t] was united with [tᶜ] rather than with [kᶜ], with both of which it is in complementary distribution, because it was more similar to [tᶜ] than to [k].

Formulation in terms of phonetic similarity also suffers from vagueness. Similarity is being used both as an absolute and as a comparative concept. In cases such as [h] and [ŋ], how similar must the sounds be in order to be judged members of the same phoneme? And what is the reasoned basis for the assertion that [tᶜ] is more similar to [t] than it is to [k]?

There had meanwhile developed in Europe, chiefly in the work of the so-called Prague school, a solution to this problem that seemed to be far more satisfactory. In basic accordance with the coordinates of nineteenth-century phonetics, a particular phone could be specified by the finite set of its phonetic features. We could then demand that the overall solution fulfill the requirement that all the phones that are assigned to the same phoneme share a set of features that is unique—that is, which differs in at least one feature from the common set of every other phoneme.

Let us apply this principle to the two problems discussed earlier. The only feature common to [h] and [ŋ] is mere consonantality, which is found in all the consonantal phones in English. Hence, if [h] and [ŋ] belong to the same phoneme, this principle would entail the absurd conclusion that there is only one consonantal phoneme in English. This can be refuted formally, within this procedure, by pointing to the many pairs of English consonants that are in minimal contrast. Therefore, [h] and [ŋ] are separate phonemes.

In the other case, if we unite [t] with [tᶜ] and with the other phones that are usually considered to be members of the English phoneme /t/, and then proceed similarly for [p], [pᶜ], and so on, and [k], [kᶜ], and so on, in accordance with the intuitively appealing solution, then each of /t/, /p/, and /k/ has a unique set of common features: (1) for /t/, voicelessness, alveolar point of articulation, stop articulation, and nonnasality; (2) for /p/, voicelessness, bilabial point of articulation, stop articulation, and nonnasality; (3) for /k/, voicelessness, velar point of articulation, stop articulation, and nonnasality. Were we to unite, say, [tᶜ] with [k], then the common features would be only voicelessness, stop articulation, and nonnasality; that set would not be unique because it also includes [t], [kᶜ], [p], and [pᶜ]. Again we are prevented from coming to such an absurd conclusion as that there is only one unvoiced nonnasal stop phoneme in English, which embraces all the variants of *p*, *t*, and *k*—this time by the presence of a number of contrasts within this set of phones.

In addition to furnishing a solution to problems of this kind, the Prague school's approach had other advantages. Since all the phones assigned to a particular phoneme had a number of features in common and this set of phones was unique, it constituted a definition of that phoneme. Thus /t/ in English would be defined by the features alveolar, unvoiced, nonnasal, stop. Since the same features reappeared, however, in other phonemes but in different combinations, the set of phonemes could be exhibited as a total structure, in which their interrelationships were specified by means of the features. Unlike the purely distributional approach, in which there was no reference to phonic content, through the utilization of features it became possible to place a particular phoneme in an overall structure and to justify the intuition that, for example, English /t/ was somehow closer to /d/ than to /m/, and that the relation of /t/ to /d/ was analogous to that of /k/ to /g/. The former followed from the fact that /t/ differs from /d/ in only one feature, voicing, while it differs from /m/ in the further features of bilabial articulation and nasality. The analogical relation $t{:}d = k{:}g$ followed from the fact that both pairs differ in exactly the same way—namely, that the first member was unvoiced and the second voiced, while each pair had all its other features in common. We see, in Table 1, this portion of the English consonantal system.

TABLE I

|  | Unvoiced Stop | Voiced Stop | Voiced Nasal |
|---|---|---|---|
| Bilabial | p | b | m |
| Alveolar | t | d | n |
| Velar | k | g | ŋ |

Those phonetic features in a particular system that were part of the definitions of the phonemes were its distinctive features. Every language utilizes only some among its phonetically possible sources of contrast, and this seems to provide a reasonable basis for comparing sound systems of different languages. Thus the intuitively recognized difference between Hindi and English in regard to aspiration can be stated succinctly in the following terms: Aspiration is a distinctive feature in the Hindi system, but not in the English system.

Prague phonological theory thus provided solutions to basic analytic problems and, in the very process of doing so, also provided a method for exhibiting the structure of individual sound systems and, at the same time, for comparing the sound systems of different languages. The theory was an impressive one, and it won broad support in Europe and eventually in the United States. Yet there remained serious problems, which centered at the very lowest and the very highest levels, so to speak: the phonetic basis for the features, and the relation of the segmental phonological units to higher-level grammatical structures.

In its classical form, Prague theory rested on the articulatory phonetics that was one of the major achievements of nineteenth-century linguistics. This body of theory, while it represented a great advance in that it provided a general framework, mainly articulatory, within which all possible human speech sounds could be placed in terms of a limited number of coordinates, was nevertheless either incomplete or imprecise in a number of important ways. In spite of occasional concerted efforts in that direction, it never succeeded in producing a truly standard and precise terminology. Moreover, the number of basic features that were required to specify all sounds had never been precisely enumerated and seemed quite large. In particular, the traditional dichotomy between vowel and consonant remained, leaving each with a practically separate body of terms, which seemed both wasteful and unsystematic. Yet there were phonetic qualities that cut across this division, some of them recognized in the current terminology, although in unsystematic fashion—for example, nasality in consonants, corresponding to nasalization in vowels. One of the results of the rapid advance in acoustic research after World War II was to add still others of this kind. Moreover, it had long been clear that the division between vowels and consonants was not absolute, that, for example, certain consonants, particularly the liquid ($r$ and $l$) sounds, were more vowellike than other consonants. The binary theory that was developed by Roman Jakobson and his associates, by using acoustic as well as articulatory evidence, provided a vast simplification: it reduced all sound differences to differences in positive or negative specification for twelve binary features.[3]

A fundamental phonetic problem to which traditional phonetics had not always given a clear-cut answer was that of the possibility of an unarbitrary division of the speech chain into phonetic segments. In particular, certain quite common classes of sounds seemed susceptible of analysis either as sequences of two segments or as single segments. Among these were diphthongs, which, since they were glides from one vocalic position to another, could be looked upon either as single segments, being unitary movements, or as complex entities, specifiable as a succession of initial and final position, with the glide between them as an inevitable and predictable concomitant. Another example of such difficulties was unvoiced aspirated stops. Here the breath that has accumulated during the closure for the stop may be released as an audible puff of air, for a perceptible period before the onset of a following voiced vowel. The aspiration may therefore be analyzed either as one aspect of the formation of the stop, in which case the aspirated stop is a single segment, or as the base of a separately audible release— that is, as a second segment, which follows the stop.

The problem is indeed a fundamental one, since the assignment of phonetic features to each segment is a necessary preliminary in this type of phonemic analysis, and the possibility of such assignment in turn presupposes an unambiguous division of the speech continuum into segments of that sort.

Once more binary theory has provided answers, in that considerations of economy on a crosslinguistic basis furnishes the motive for adopting one or another alternative as a generalized solution. This does produce the danger, of course, that on analysis one alternative may be imposed that runs counter to the one that is otherwise preferable for a given language, or else runs counter to an otherwise valid crosslinguistic generalization.

Another source of difficulty that is inherent in traditional articulatory phonetics is what might be called its static positional nature. Every segment is defined in terms of the place and type of constriction of the speech organs. Thus a *t* sound is defined as an unvoiced nonnasal alveolar stop, translatable into something like the following: a complete closure with abrupt release (*stop*) by the tongue against the alveolar ridge (*alveolar*), with raising of the velic to shut off the egress of air through the nasal resonance chamber (*nonnasalized*), while the glottis remains open (*unvoiced*). The transitions (*glides*) from one position to another are assumed to be predictable, of short duration and without any appreciable acoustic effect. Doubt has been cast on these assumptions by developments in acoustic phonetics.[4] Moreover, relations among segments of the speech chain that are not seen as inherent in any segment, when it is viewed statically and in isolation, are not easily integrated into the theory. For example, viewed statically, [i] is a high, front unrounded, voiced sound without audible friction and hence is traditionally considered to be a vowel. When it is more prominent, for one or another reason, than surrounding sounds, it functions as the peak of a syllable; under these circumstances, it is usually regarded as a vowel and assigned to a phoneme symbolized as /i/. When it is less prominent than surrounding sounds, even though its static formation may be identical, it may be the margin instead of the center of a syllable, like the initial sound of the English word *yard*. Syllabic function, then, just like pitch, stress, duration, and certain other features, involves relations among different members of the same speech continuum.

The rules for the occurrence of such relational features have frequently required reference to longer grammatically defined units, such as the word, the clause, or the sentence. In Prague phonology, the word in particular was taken for granted as the reference point for phonological rules. Thus, for a language like Czech, in which, according to the traditional terminology, every word was stressed on the first syllable, Prague doctrine would call stress predictable and therefore nonphonemic. The rule for its occurrence could be stated only if one already knew the word boundaries. Yet these boundaries themselves were not marked by any specific phonetic characteristics other than this very occurrence of stress on the first syllable. Prague theory thus took word boundaries for granted, as being supplied presumably by grammatical analysis.

In the United States, an attempt was made to deal with such problems by the notion of the boundaries (*junctures*) themselves as being phonological units, which served as conditioning factors for the operation of rules concerning relational features distributed over words and other longer grammatically relevant units. These junctures were remarkable in that they had no inherent phonetic features, but revealed themselves only as conditioning factors for other phonemes. They were justified in terms of economy. For example, if a juncture phoneme as word boundary were not admitted in Czech, stress would become phonemic and the number of vowel phonemes doubled, since to every unstressed vowel there would now correspond a stressed vowel phoneme. The appeal to economy, however, tells us merely that this is a scientifically desirable solution. We still need units without any phonetic features, the positing of which was originally motivated by reference to a grammatically rather than phonologically defined segment.

Another typically recurrent situation was one in which a complex and phonetically rather arbitrary phonemic analysis appealed to analysts of a particular language because of morphophonemic considerations that were basically grammatical. Gleason cites a form of Swahili in which a particular segment β (a voiced bilabial fricative), is statistically rare.[5] It occurs precisely at those places where, on grammatical grounds, a sequence *bw* would be expected. There is in Swahili a verb passive suffix formant -*w*-, for example, *kat-a* (to cut), *kat-w-a* (to be cut). The passive of *iba* (to steal), is, however, not \**ib-w-a*, as would be expected, but *iβa*.[6] The phonetic segment [β] is therefore analyzed as representing the phonemic sequence /bw/. This recommends itself for reasons of economy, which have proven in general to be irresistible to analysts of specific languages. By such decisions we have one less phoneme, that is, /β/, at the same time as we simplify grammatical statements such as those having to do with the passive in Swahili. The cost is an additional allophonic rule—a cost that seemed particularly small to those to whom allophones were not even part of the language as such, but rather belonged to *parole*. There was, however, the additional implication for theory that, if such solutions were employed—and in practice they were—we had once more used grammatical considerations in phonology and had thus destroyed the chances of defining each phoneme in terms of a set of exclusive relevant features. In the above case, for example, every other allophone of *b* was a stop, a feature that distinguished *b* from *w*. But if [β] represents /bw/, then the most we can say is that the fricative closure of [β] is midway between the stop of other occurrences of /b/ and the nonfrictional closure of other examples of /w/.

This situation exists because a former sequence, which was phonetically [bw], has changed to β, which has retained, given the recency of the change, the distributional characteristics of the former sequence [bw]. If we analyze β as /bw/, then the language has changed only phonetically. If we do not do so, then the change is "structural" and a new phoneme /β/ has resulted. What is real is the change.

This brings to the fore a fundamental problem. Phonemic theory in general involves, as we have seen, two kinds of considerations: functional (distributional) and material (phonetic). The functional relationships between similar

sounds that are typically both viewed by the speakers themselves as allophonic and analyzed as such by the most universally accepted phonemic procedures, are those that result
from certain types of regular sound change as an historical
process. Let us take the case of unconditioned sound change,
in which all occurrences of a particular sound $x$ are replaced
by another sound $y$. Such a replacement, like that of $t$ by $d$
in some languages, does not, as we have seen in a previous
chapter, take place instantaneously. For many speakers, the
older forms in $t$ exist side by side with the innovative forms
in $d$, for all occurrences of the former $t$. In such cases every
meaningful element (for example, morpheme) that has a $t$,
for example, *tan* (to weave) has an alternant *dan*. The
speaker uses either one or the other without any apparent
regularity to his choice—a phenomenon that we have called
*free variation.*

Clearly, at this point $t$ and $d$ have the same environments distributionally and the variation does not serve
to distinguish one message from another. On functional
grounds, therefore, there can be no stronger case than the
one for free variants being allophones of the same phoneme.
Yet the possibility of analyzing these as members of the
same phoneme, when we require phonetic common features
for all allophones, is dependent on the nature of historic
change. This is normally such that the earlier and later
sounds are phonetically similar, so that they usually have
common phonetic features. But it is not always possible
to have one's functional cake while eating it. For example,
the change $s > h$ is fairly common, but phonetically are
so dissimilar that it is unlikely that the features they have
in common will be unique to them. Since this change is
widely attested from historical records, however, it is not
surprising that, for example, certain forms of Caribbean
Spanish at present have $s$ and $h$ in free variation in certain
environments. In such cases having the functional cake will
probably seem preferable, since the refusal to regard $s$ and
$h$ as members of the same phoneme is motivated only by the

desire to save a dogma that, for reasons already described, must be abandoned anyway.

We conclude from this part of our discussion that phonology cannot be an entirely autonomous part of linguistic description and that the attempt to set up a discrete set of phonemic units, based on common phonetic features and the absence of contrast, cannot be successfully carried through. Hence the integration of phonology into the total grammar, which would allow us to specify higher-level relational features by reference to grammatical units, as advocated by the transformationalists, is a fundamentally necessary step.

# VI

## LINGUISTIC CHANGE

Until this point, the discussion has dealt with the requirements for a scientifically adequate description of particular forms of speech ("languages") during a specified chronological period and in abstraction from change—that is, it has been concerned with individual synchronic descriptions. But a basic aim of scientific linguistics, as it is of any science, is to uncover regularities and significant relationships within its subject matter in the most general sense, and this requires the systematic use of comparative methods. Several major types of comparative studies are in fact capable of contributing toward the goal of generalizations about language. The first of these is historical linguistics proper—the comparison of different time states of the same language.[1]

Just as the formulation of generalizing statements is the aim of descriptive linguistics, so in historical linguistics the attempt is made to produce comprehensive general formulations that will connect the linguistic facts of different chronological stages of the same language. This can be accomplished reasonably well through the traditional vocabulary of process, which not only lends itself to overall statements of change for particular language histories, but has also proven, from all indications, to have universal applicability. Thus, it can be employed in the higher-level comparative study of historically unrelated instances of the same process, and thereby become an instrument for the discovery of generalizations about change.

Given the limited scope of the present work, we shall be concerned chiefly with phonological change, for a number of reasons. These include the relative ease of formulation of comprehensive processual statements, as compared with other aspects of language change, plus the fact that questions about the interconnections between diachronic process generalizations and synchronic universals lend themselves to especially clear treatment on the phonologic level.

If we compare two or more time stages of the same language, the obvious point of departure would seem to be the existence of linguistic forms—that is, of particular sound sequences with their meanings—that have persisted in recognizable form from the earlier to the later period. If, for example, we compare Anglo-Saxon with modern English, it is natural to regard the contemporary English *stone* as the modified continuation of the Anglo-Saxon form *stān* (stone). Side by side with such continuity with modification, there is, of course, much in present-day English that cannot thus be connected with earlier forms and much, on the other hand, in earlier English that has not persisted into the present. Furthermore, there are important changes, such as those in the order of elements in a construction, that are not statable in terms of the equation of earlier and later stages of the same forms. Nevertheless, the systematic treatment of cases of formal persistence provides a basic point of departure for a more comprehensive treatment of change.

There is at present no recognized term for instances of the type *stone* > *stān*. In instances in which, in several related languages, a form has persisted in the same fashion as the continuation of an earlier form in the common source language—for example, English *stone*, German *stein*, Dutch *steen*, as the reflexes of Proto-Germanic *stain-az*—the term *cognate* is in common use. In the present context, the expression *internal cognate* will be applied when the related forms are from different time stages of the same language. In that respect, Anglo-Saxon *stān* and modern English *stone* are internal cognates.

For the moment, let us approach the task of describing change by restricting it to this limited but highly important area of internal cognates. Let us assume, ideally, that we have a catalogue of such persisting forms, each entry of which consists of a set of ordered forms, pairs in the special case of only two time states being involved—for example *stān* (stone), *stewn* (stone), or *hūs* (house), *haws* (house). Sometimes, of course, the meaning will be different—for example, *hlāf* (bread), *ləwf* (loaf).

An initial atomistic approach would give sound and meaning conversion statements, for each individual case, from the earlier to the later form. Thus, in the first example cited above, it seems reasonable to assume that earlier $\bar{a}$ is converted to modern $əw$ and to put this in the form of a conversion statement $\bar{a} \rightarrow əw$. In fact, such equations as early $s$ to later $s$ ($s \rightarrow s$) are merely limiting cases of such conversions, the identity conversion $s \rightarrow s$ which also occurs for the meanings *stone* → *stone*.[2] It appears that our conversion statements are of two distinct kinds, those that refer to sound and those that refer to meaning; on the surface at least, these appear to be independent of each other and to differ in nature. For the moment we confine ourselves to sound conversions, since it turns out that this type is to a high degree susceptible of generalization.

If we consider the single conversion statement $a \rightarrow əw$ in abstraction from the specific example of *stān/stəwn*, we find it recurring in many other sets in our list—for example, *rāp/rəwp* (rope), *bān/bəwn* (bone), *bāt/bəwt* (boat), and many others. Indeed, this occurs so commonly that it is reasonable to entertain the general hypothesis that, whenever an Anglo-Saxon form has [ā], its internal cognate in modern English has [əw]. It thus becomes possible to state the conversion rule in general terms, without reference to individual sets in the list. Statements in this generalized form have traditionally been called *regular sound changes,* or even *sound laws.*

The example given is not representative, however, in one respect. It is by no means true that the earlier sound always changes to the later one. This does hold in the present instance, however, the change being of a type that is usually called unconditioned. Rather more commonly, however, certain specifiable conditions must be present in order for the change to occur. Thus, most often Anglo-Saxon ī is converted to Modern English *aj* in internal cognates—for example, *fīf/fajv* (five), *rīdan/rajd* (ride), and so forth. But this does not hold in all cases. For example, we have *fīfta/fifþ* (fifth), not modern *\*fajfþ,* and *wīsdom/wizdəm* (wisdom), not modern *\*wajzdom.* An examination of these last and other cases shows the presence of a common factor —namely, that *i* is followed by two consonants. Evidently Anglo-Saxon ī yields *i* when it is followed by two consonants, *aj* under other circumstances. When the rule has thus to be stated with explicit mention of the environments in which it holds, we have a conditioned sound change. Clearly, unconditioned change is merely a limiting case, one in which the change occurs under all conditions.

The examples just cited, in which Anglo-Saxon ī yields modern *i* rather than *aj,* illustrates certain other considerations. These cases would not usually be described as two different outcomes of Anglo-Saxon ī in Modern English; instead, it would be noted that Anglo-Saxon ī is the usual ancestor of Modern English *i.* It is, therefore, reasonable to state the correspondence between the *i* of *fīfta* and the *i* of *fifþ* not directly, but as the outcome of two conversion statements ordered in time. Anglo-Saxon ī > i before two consonants, and then /i/ of whatever origin is converted to

/i/ in Modern English. Naturally we look for evidences of this sequence of conversion statements in texts of the appropriate period; yet, even if such texts were not available, the modern outcomes would still be described in terms of such chronologically ordered rules.

This assumption is further strengthened by an examination of the historical development of the vowel system as a whole, since all long vowels in Anglo-Saxon seem to have undergone an analogous shortening before two consonants. This would tell against assuming, for example, that first Anglo-Saxon $\bar{\imath}$ became *aj* unconditionally and *aj* then became *i* before two consonants, since to do so would isolate this change from the analogous case $\bar{u} > u$, and so on.

This example suggests that statements of sound changes can sometimes be made in even more generalized form than as individual phoneme changes, abstracted from the particular examples in which they occur. By the use of sound features, the changes $\bar{\imath} > i$, $\bar{u} > u$, $\bar{a} > a$, and so on, can be described as the single change by which, in long vowels, the feature of length was replaced by that of shortness whenever the next two sounds had the general feature of consonantality. Traditional historical linguistics does in fact often employ equivalent terminology without considering the theoretical foundation for such generalizations as being based on features, and without carrying out the generalization to the fullest extent possible. Thus, no historical grammar, even if it did state the changes $\bar{\imath} > i$ in isolation from other cases of vowel shortening, would list all the two-phoneme consonant sequences that actually do occur, but would instead generalize in terms of the single highly general feature of consonantality.

When successive time stages of the same language are documented, it is not merely that certain generalizing statements of the type $\bar{a} > \partial w$ become possible. Such conclusions are not isolated achievements; rather, the chronologically ordered set of conditioned and unconditioned conversion rules accounts for the totality of sounds in the later members

of internal cognate sets by way of applications of these conversion rules to the sounds of the earlier set. Conversely,
every sound in the earlier set figures in the conversion rules,
so that its regular outcomes under specified conditions are
already known. This is an ideal, of course, but it is, in fact,
attainable, as a rule, if we make allowance for a relatively
small number of marginal uncertainties.

Such rubrics as conditioned and unconditioned regular
change are useful not only for stating in comprehensive
terms the changes that have been undergone by a particular
language during the course of the historical development
of its sound system; they also have universal applicability
on a comparative basis. Whenever internal cognates, specified in terms of the universally valid categories of phonetic
description, are examined with care, it turns out that conversion statements of regular sound change can be derived.
We may regard regular conditioned and unconditioned
change as *processes,* meaning by this term classes of changes
with definable similarities that can be observed in historically independent cases. Such processes can be classified
in various ways into subprocesses that are dependent on
more delimited characteristics. Thus, the change of any
sound in any language to some other sound, under specified
phonetic conditions, can be regarded as an individual instance of the same very general class of changes, the process
of regular conditioned sound change. But much more specific subclasses can be distinguished, which recur in historically independent cases and can thus be considered comparable. For example, the unconditional unrounding of
rounded front vowels that is found in the change from Old
English *y* and *ȳ* (phonetically *ü* and *ü:*) to *i* and *i:* respectively, may be regarded as a specific subprocess; similar
examples are known in German dialects, in the early modern
Greek change of *ü* (written upsilon) to *i*, and elsewhere.
Hence, such categories enable us to proceed to the comparative study of change and open up possibilities for universal

conclusions about diachronic process, which will be considered in detail in Chapter IX.

It is almost always the case that a certain number of internal cognates do not follow the general rules of conditioned and unconditioned sound changes. But an examination of these cases will generally show that they are not in the main random exceptions. Nearly all of them fall under a number of types, each of which may be regarded as a sporadic process rather than a general process, the term *sporadic* here merely indicating that our conversion statements involve the listing of specific forms rather than the generalizing formulations that are characteristic of sound laws.[3] This is justified by the fact that the deviant cases cluster into well-defined groups and on the grounds that similar groupings appear in the most diverse languages during the course of changes in those languages. It follows, then, that these are processes in the sense defined earlier, in that they are classes of similar changes.

Since it is not my purpose here to offer an exhaustive analysis of processes of change, only a few representative types will be considered. Among the deviant cases, it will usually be found that a considerable number involve two classes of consonantal sounds, the *sonants* (liquids and nasals) and, less prominently, the *sibilants*. That this is not a mere chance matter is shown by the fact that all or almost all of these are found in forms that contain in their earlier appearance two or more occurrences within one of the two classes of sounds just mentioned. Typical examples of sporadic changes of sonants are the following. In Spanish, the Vulgar Latin *anma* (Classical *anima*) (soul) became *alma*—that is, the first of the two nasals became a liquid. Likewise in Spanish, the Latin *arbor*, which contains two occurrences of the liquid *r*, becomes *arbol*. An example from a different language stock is Aramaic (Semitic) *tarten* (two) from earlier *\*tanten;* here the earlier form contains the sonant *n* twice; in this instance, the first *n* is changed to a different sonant, namely *r*. Another example, from Tigrinya, a Semitic language of Ethiopia—namely, *alama* from earlier *anama* (to weave)—is strikingly parallel to the Spanish example *alma* < *anma* (soul).

In all these cases, we are not dealing with general sound laws; for example, in the instance of Spanish *alma* < *anma*, it is not a regular rule that, wherever in Vulgar Latin *n* is followed by *m*, it is replaced by *l*. Further, these changes have a number of common characteristics, in addition to their sporadicity, that distinguish them as a group from the regular conditioned sound changes with which they might most reasonably be compared. Whereas the conditioning factor in regular changes almost always either follows or precedes immediately, in these changes there is often action at a distance (e.g., in a*r*bo*r* > a*r*bo*l*). Furthermore, in a clear majority of cases, regular conditioned change is anticipatory, in that the conditioning factor follows rather than precedes the sound that is changed. Thus, in the example cited earlier of the shortening of vowels in late Anglo-Saxon, the conditioning element is the fact that two consonants follow immediately. In the sporadic changes, however, the proportion of perseverative changes—those in which the conditioning factor precedes—is quite considerable; for example, Spanish *arbol*, in which the second rather than the first *r* of Latin *arbor* has changed. Finally, we may point to a conspicuous difference in the two kinds of changes: Regular change is almost always assimilatory— that is, the new sound is phonetically more similar to the conditioning factor than the replaced sound; in the sporadic changes, by contrast, the resulting sound is frequently more unlike the conditioning sound than the older one was. For example, a typical regular conditioned sound change that shows assimilation is the Latin shift of *n* to *m* before a following *p* or *b*—for example, *impossibilis* (impossible) from *in* + *possibilis*, and *impellere* (to impel) from *inpellere*. Here the replacing sound *m* is more like *p* than *n* is, since it shares with *p* the factor of bilabial articulation. On the other hand, in the sporadic change of Spanish *arbol* < *arbor,* the earlier sequence of two phonetically identical *r* sounds is destroyed through replacement of one of these by an *l.*

This suggests that the distinction between these two processes has psychological as well as descriptive significance. The sporadic changes of sonants and sibilants involve associative interference at a distance and constitute a "higher-level" psychological process than the more directly physiological adjustment of neighboring sounds that underlies regular conditioned sound changes.

A further example of a sporadic type of change is morphological analogy. This is a very important process in the historical development of language: probably the largest number of instances in which an internal cognate does not take the form anticipated in accordance with the regular sound laws are referable to this source.

The situation in which analogical changes arise is precipitated by the regular operation of conditioned sound changes. Where a particular meaningful element (morpheme) appears in a number of differing environments, some of which contain the conditioning factor and some of which do not, the originally uniform morpheme will take on two phonetically different forms. For example, in the development of Italian from Latin, *k,* by a conditioned regular change, became *č* before the vowels *e, i;* but remained *k* before *a, o,* and *u.* Hence in the word for *friend* the singular is *amik-o* but the plural *amič-i;* and in the verb *to say* we have *dik-o* (I say) and *dik-a* (say)—polite imperative— but *dič-i* (thou sayest) and *dič-evo* (I was saying). This is indeed the way in which morphological irregularities typically came into existence. An important counterprocess, which tends to restore regularity, is analogy. Thus, in the Italian word for *fig,* the same sound laws would lead us to expect the singular *fik-o* and the plural *\*fič-i,* yet the plural is actually *fik-i.* Since regular cases are to be found in which alternation does not occur, this type of change is often stated by means of a so-called analogical proportion—for example, *nas-o:nas-i = fik-o:x,* where the form *fik-i* is to be supplied for *x*. Of course, any of very many regular pairs in Italian—not only *naso* (nose), as in the present example—could have been utilized for the left side of the proportion. It is not maintained that any particular set furnished the actual model.

Analogy is capable of being, and is in fact the chief factor, in eliminating the irregularities that are produced by regular conditioned sound change. Nevertheless, it does not always and of necessity lead to changes that enhance the degree of morphological regularity in the language. Instead, analogical change may result in the extension of less frequent patterns or of those that involve greater variation in the alternating morphemes. Thus, although the general trend in the history of the English language has been for the analogical spread of the weak "regular" type of conjugation—for example, present *call*, preterite *called*, past participle *called*—there are instances of the spread of statistically infrequent and irregular patterns, as in the past *dived*, which has been largely replaced in present-day English by *dove*. For in analogical change we often have a number of possible models, at the least two, since each analogy could go either way. For *dove* we might set up as an analogical proportion *strive:strove = dive:x*. The "opposite" proportion *dive:dived =strive:x* would have produced *strived*, but in this case it was not followed. While the classification of certain cases as analogical is an indispensable first step, it remains to be seen whether any general principles can be found that underlie the actualization of certain possible analogies and the nonfunctioning of others.

Analogy qualifies as a sporadic process in that individual morphemes must be referred to in describing it. Psychologically, we may reasonably consider it as a still higher-level process than that which is involved in the sporadic sound changes described earlier since, by contrast with sporadic or regular sound changes, the relevant associative forms do not occur in the utterance that is changed. For example, *dived* is affected by the present *dive*, with its resemblance to *strive* and thus by the preterite of the latter verb, even though none of these presumably occurred in the sentences in which *dived* was replaced by *dove;* in the dissimilation of *arbor* to *arbol*, however, the second *r* was affected by the presence of a preceding *r* in the actual speech chain.

The concept of analogy has been applied here in a rather restricted sense: It has been confined to those instances in which an analogical proportion is constructible. Sometimes the term is used more broadly. For example, in Old Church Slavonic, two of the masculine declensions, the *o*-stems and *u*-stems, had already partially fallen together. As a result of this situation, Serbian inherited two inflectional endings in the nominative plural, *-i* from the *o*-stems and *-ove* from the *u*-stems; the second of these was subsequently changed to *-ovi*, as it is sometimes stated, "on the analogy of the ending *-i*." But in such a case, no analogical proportion is actually available; rather, it falls under the broad rubric of contamination—in this instance, the contamination of one allomorph *-ove* by another *-i*, which produced *ovi* in place of *ove*.

A number of other processes of this same general type might be similarly distinguished; but, until now, as compared with the area of sound change proper, exact analysis of them has been largely neglected.

A summary of the main forces that come into play in the development of morphological systems reveals their heterogeneity and complexity. We have already seen that sound change in the form of conditioned regular changes, while it is, strictly speaking, a factor external to morphology as such, produces morphological irregularity. Nor is this the only effect produced by sound change. Regular mergers, by which all or a conditioned subset of occurrences of a particular sound coalesce with some other sound, may erase previous alternation or may either partly or completely collapse category distinctions. Thus, the change of all final unstressed vowels except *-i* to a single vowel *-a*, along with the change of final -*m* to -*n* which was then followed by the loss of -*n*, destroyed the distinction between the nominative, dative, and accusative cases in the transition from Anglo-Saxon to Middle English.

Not all change in morphological systems is produced by the interplay of phonetic and analogical-type processes. For example, the original dual number in the noun has disappeared as a distinct category in almost all Indo-European languages. This was not, by and large, due to the fact that dual endings merged by phonetic change, or that they were analogically remodeled after those of the other members, singular and plural. It was rather that the plural replaced the dual in those contexts in which the dual had formerly appeared. In a few instances, in languages in which the dual form was particularly frequent—for example, in words like *eye* and *ear*—it was the dual form that replaced the corresponding plural. This process may be regarded as semantic, in that the morphemes of the plural changed their meaning from "more than two" to "more than one," and the semantic category "two" in nominal declension was eliminated. There was an overall regularity to this process, in that it was always the plural that merged with the dual, never the singular. If the latter had occurred in any Indo-European language, the result would have been a noun system with two categories: one with the meaning of "at least two," the other "more than two." It seems that no such system is known, either in Indo-European languages or anywhere else in the world.

Sometimes a morphological category is eliminated in an even more drastic manner. Thus, the genitive case of Classical Latin was replaced in Vulgar Latin by the preposition *dē* (originally *from* with the ablative), and this is the source of the genitive expressions that are current in the western Romance languages. In this instance, we may say that the morphological system has been restructured through semantic change: an extension in the meaning of *dē*, by which the old inflected genitive was replaced in all its usages and disappeared.

In considering morphological change, we have already begun to move beyond the method of internal cognates, which proved so useful for generalizing in regard to phonological change. For one thing, the tacit limitation on cognates, as involving a one-to-one relation between the set of earlier forms and that of later forms, does not hold here. Rather the relation is many-to-one, with a single modern form resulting from the coalescence by phonetic change of originally distinct earlier forms. For example, the Modern English *son* continues various originally distinct case forms of the Anglo-Saxon *sunu*—for example, the nominative singular *sunu*, the dative singular *suna*, and the accusative singular *sunu*—so that nominative *sunu/son* and dative *suna/son* can be regarded as two distinct internal cognates.

In the case of the Romance genitive, we have taken a further step, since it makes sense from the historical point of view to say that the Latin inflected form has been replaced by the construction of the noun with the preposition *dē*, yet the latter is not a continuation of the former, in any reasonable sense of *internal cognate*. The persistence is rather that of function only (the genitive meaning), which is expressed by two unconnected formal means in different stages of the history of the Romance languages. True, we can subsume this under two conversion statements: one connects earlier *dē* on the restricted meaning *from* with later *dē* in its more extended meaning; the second, by the device of zero as a limiting notion, states that the old genitive case morpheme of Latin is replaced by zero (i.e., disappears). It may be added parenthetically that, by the use of zero, we could incorporate obsolescences (replaced by zero) and new creations (arise by zero) into the overall framework. In the present instance, the employment of two disconnected statements—the semantic expansion of *dē* and the obsolescence of the inflected genitive—fails to convey the essence of the process, which is the functional replacement of the latter by the former.

Again, a further but not unnatural extension of the notion of internal cognate would be necessary in order to cover certain processes of syntactic change—for example, in word order. Thus, in one stage of the history of a language, the order of elements in some construction may be free, while later on, one of the alternatives becomes fixed as a norm. For example, in Vulgar Latin one could place the article *ille* either before or after the noun, while in Western Romance languages the former order eventually became fixed. Then we might say that Latin *homo ille* (Italian *l'uomo*), and Latin *ille homo* (Italian *l'uomo*), are both internal cognates; the comparison of many such sets will thus lead to a generalization in regard to change of word order. Another example of how a syntactic change can be fitted into this overall pattern is the following. In earlier English, it was not possible to say such things as *the mailbox at the corner, the man in the house*. These apparently developed as abbreviations of the relative clause *the mailbox that is at the corner, the man who is in the house*. The relation between the two is stated in modern transformational grammars, which derive such phrases as *the mailbox at the corner* by a *deletion transformation* from *the mailbox that is at the corner*. In terms of internal cognates, we would have a one-to-many relation between the earlier and later forms, in contrast to the many-to-one relationship of *ille homo* and *homo ille* to *l'uomo*. Thus, the earlier *the mailbox that is at the corner* is continued by both *the mailbox that is at the corner* and *the mailbox at the corner*. A generalization of the latter members of such pairs leads to conceiving of the deletion as an historical change, rather than as a synchronic grammatical relation.

These last instances, in which phrases, rather than individual word forms, figure in the conversion statements, differ from the earlier examples in another essential way.

In word conversion statements of the type *stān/stone, bān/ bone*, the list is finite, whereas relative clauses of the type *the mailbox that is on the corner* belong to an infinite set. For example, the initial noun in this phrase can have an un- limited number of adjectival modifiers—*the red mailbox that is on the corner, the large red mailbox that is on the corner*, and so on. In practice, this produces a real difference in the procedures of the historical linguist: in the finite case, he examines each internal cognate in search of generalizing statements, such as those that are embodied in regular sound changes; in the latter case, given the infinity of the sets and the relative rarity with which one encounters the exact descendant form in any individual case, it is rather rules that are compared. Thus, in traditional comparative linguistics, in regard to adjective-noun order in the Romance languages, change is normally stated in terms of a change of rule.

The question at issue is the metalanguage for the de- scription of change. It may either refer directly to the lin- guistic phenomena, or it may refer to the statements in the grammatical descriptions. This latter possibility has been brought into prominence by recent theories of generative grammar, which would presumably seek to describe all change by conversion statements between grammars rather than by linguistic events. As we have seen, traditional his- torical linguistics employs both approaches: the former in syntax, an infinite domain; the latter in phonology, a finite domain. Its conceptualizations have grown up, however, in random fashion: no overall theoretical basis for the descrip- tion of change has ever been developed.

One important area of linguistic change has not yet been discussed, that of change in lexical meaning. In the initial section of this chapter, we saw that systematic com- parison of the phonetic shapes of the internal cognates leads to the generalizing statements known as regular sound changes. A corresponding study of meanings does not, how- ever, lead to this same result. There is no known method by which, as in the phonetic domain, a subset of internal cognates with some defining characteristic can be subject to the same basic process in order to produce the later members of the pairs. In the light of the factors involved in semantic change, the search for such "laws" seems groundless and has, indeed, been generally abandoned.

At the same time, semantic changes do fall into certain general types and do show certain resemblances in historically independent cases. Indeed, this is so much the case that we have here almost an *embarras de richesse* of more or less systematic and partly disparate modes of classification. In this is reflected the still uncertain status of descriptive semantics.

In order to illustrate such a classification, we may take what is probably the simplest one, the so-called logical mode. In its narrowest form, it would classify changes merely in terms of the logical relations of inclusion and exclusion of the class of designata, before and after the change. Thus, the Old English word *dēor,* which once meant *animal,* in general came to mean *deer* in Modern English. Since the class of deer is contained in the class of animals, this is an example of narrowing. The change of Old English *fugel* (bird) to its modern meaning of *fowl* is an example of the same process. Each case, however, would have to be listed separately, since there is no overall semantic characteristic of all the earlier forms that underwent narrowing, nor, indeed, is there any general rule from which we could deduce such specific narrowings as *deer, fowl,* and so on.

It is obvious that, in semantic change, the connection between changes that involve different conversion rules yet are fundamentally connected will be particularly important. Thus, given *dēor* (animal) > *dijr* (deer), it is natural to inquire whether the old meaning *animal,* now no longer covered by *dēor,* was at that time provided for, and how. These considerations have led to field or configurational historical studies, in which the overall field to be investigated is defined semantically and its changes of organization over time are studied with particular attention to the discovery of the social and cultural factors that may have been involved in such shifts.

One important group of processes that is always included in conventional discussions has not yet been mentioned. These are the changes attributable to the influence of other languages; the chief example of this is borrowing. They introduce a new external causal dimension, independent of the purely internal considerations involved throughout the previous discussion, which are rather based on comparison of two or more time stages of the same language, without reference to other languages as sources of change. In principle, the influence of some other language might, in some instances, be demonstrated, with greater or lesser plausibility, to be operative in any of the processes thus far discussed. Thus, it has been pointed out that the sound changes in neighboring languages often tend to produce convergent results. For example, it may be argued, with some justice, that it is not accidental that the only Slavonic languages that have vowel quantity, Czech and Slovak, border on Hungarian, which has the same feature. In such cases, the changes by which vowel quantity developed in Czech and Slovak are regarded as examples of regular sound change; the possible influence of Hungarian is then regarded as a separate causal factor. Where the evidence is quite indisputable, however, as in the borrowing of words with sound and meaning similar to that in the source language, a separate processual name, *borrowing*, is used. If we compared the language at earlier and later stages without consideration of the external source, we would call this a *coinage*—that is, a new lexical item without historical antecedents in the language. Thus several of the more common types of change in which foreign influence is easy to detect have received separate names, depending on the presence or absence of a provable external factor in their genesis.

Here, too, a sound instinct is being followed, in that historically independent cases can be classified under the same type and a comparative study becomes possible of such questions as which aspects of language are most typically open to foreign influence and what modifications they are subject to when adopted.

In later discussion, it will be shown that, in spite of their lack of overall rationalization, the traditional process categories in which linguistic changes are stated make possible fruitful comparison and generalization.

# VII

## TYPES OF LANGUAGE CLASSIFICATION

In the previous chapter, only one type of comparative study was considered, that which involved direct historical comparison of different time stages of the same language. Like all systematic comparison, this led to classification, for in comparing we note similarities and differences, and the possession of similarities then becomes the basis for assignment to the same category. In direct historical comparison, the conceptualization was in terms of processes as classes of similar changes, so that it was changes that were classified.[1] In other types of comparative studies now to be considered, it is the languages themselves rather than changes in them that are the objects of classification.

Direct historical comparison may be regarded as a special and limiting case of the more general method of comparative-historical investigation, in which the historical continuity among the languages being compared is not confined (as it is in the direct method) to the single time relation (earlier-to-later). In a speech community of any considerable geographic extent, there develop regional variants (*local dialects*)—particularly if migration or the intervention of a foreign group splits the community into segments that do not communicate with one another. Eventually, unless linguistic unity is restored by the spread of a single dominant dialect, such dialects become more and more different, until they reach the point at which we can reasonably say that mutual intelligibility no longer exists. We now speak of related but separate languages, rather than of dialects of the same language.

The best attested case, historically speaking, is that of the origin of the contemporary Romance local dialects and standard languages by differentiation from colloquial Latin. Again, the earlier forms of the present-day German languages—Old High German, Old Saxon, Anglo-Saxon and Old Norse—resemble each other far more than do the present-day languages; at the earliest period at which they were recorded, they could almost be regarded as dialectical variants of the same language.

Two somewhat oversimplified metaphors are current in describing the relationships that arise in this way: that of the branching tree and that of the genealogical table. The two metaphors are really equivalent, their common feature being the notion of repeated branching. Once a dialect has acquired the status of a separate language, it is itself subject to the process of dialectal split and to the ultimate production of new and distinct languages.

The example of the Romance languages and Latin, cited above, is in one respect unrepresentative. In most instances the ancestral language is not represented directly by written records. It is usual under these circumstances to coin terms with the prefix *Proto-*. Thus the ancestral Germanic language, which is not directly available in written form, is called Proto-Germanic.

A classification in accordance with the principle of the family tree is often called a *genetic* classification. Every node, or branching point, in such a diagram represents a formerly existing language, whether or not it is known from written records; all the languages that have descended from some single nodal language constitute a genetic group. Thus, the total set of Indo-European languages is a genetic group because these are all the languages that go back to one node (Proto-Indo-European). The Germanic languages likewise constitute a genetic group. But the group of languages that includes English, German, French, and Albanian is not a genetic group, since its only common ancestor is Proto-Indo-European and there are many other Indo-European languages besides these four. On the other hand, these languages can be said to be *related*, a term that is used about two or more languages that have a demonstrated common ancestral language, at however great a remove. The possibility of varying degrees of relationship is also implied by this scheme. If the common node between language A and language C is farther back than the common node of A and B, then A is more closely related to B than it is to C. For example, English is more closely related to German than it is to French, because its common node with German (Proto-Germanic) is less remote than its common node with French (Indo-European).

The value of genetic classification is so evident that when the phrase *language classification* is used without qualification, it is usually this kind that is meant. Genetic classification provides the foundation for historical-comparative linguistics, whose basic task has been the reconstruction of ancestral languages—for example, Proto-Indo-European— by systematic comparison of the descendant languages. In the performance of this task, the main assumptions have been of the processual type noted in the previous chapter; that is, the question of the nature of the protolanguage has been couched mainly in the following terms: What must have been the characteristics of the protolanguage so that it could have developed, by known types of processes, into the various descendant languages? It is not within the scope of this study to discuss the elaborate techniques that have been devised in comparative linguistics to carry out this inquiry. For our present purposes, we may note that, to a very considerable extent, what is known about specific changes in language is provided by this method, which thus supplements the direct historical method.

The importance of the comparative-historical approach is not confined to the history of language itself. Much valuable historical information of a nonlinguistic sort can be derived from linguistic reconstructions. Further, as compared with the other major types of linguistic classification to be discussed later, this approach is nonarbitrary and definite. In principle, only one correct genetic classification can exist, and it is intimately connected with actual historical events—namely, the differentiation over time of originally uniform speech communities. It is, therefore, nonarbitrary. It is also definite, in the sense that every language is in principle unambiguously assignable to a specific genetic group.

Other types of classification exist, however, that have their own legitimacy and value. There is no need, as has often been true in the past, to conceive of these various methods of classification as rival theories; they are all logically compatible with one another. For example, there is no contradiction involved in stating that, genetically, Rumanian is a Romance language and therefore belongs with French, Italian, Spanish, Portuguese, and so on, and at the same time that it belongs to an areally defined Balkan group of languages, on the basis of which it will be classified with such languages as Bulgarian, Albanian, and Greek, which belong to genetically different branches of Indo-European. Areal classification is based on an estimate that, on the dimension of external diachronic process, of which the most easily detectable instances are borrowings, a particular group of languages have through contact developed common features that distinguish them from the languages of other geographical areas.

Thus, the historical processes involved in the two modes of classification are different. There is also a chronological factor, in that the resemblances attributed to contact are more recent than those that result from genetic common origin. Not only is there no contradiction involved in the simultaneous assignment of a language to genetic and areal groups with distinct memberships; on occasion, specific historical developments can also be viewed without contradiction as internal genetic developments that have been causally induced by external factors. Thus, the development of vowel length in Czech is on the one hand statable as a regular development from the earlier inherited Slavic sound system, while at the same time it is possible to maintain that this particular development would not have occurred in the absence of contact with Hungarian, a neighboring, non-Indo-European language.

In the examples of Czech and Rumanian, we have illustrated a further method of language classification, the *areal*. Areal groupings are clearly historical; they are in principle similar to the "culture area" classifications that have been established by anthropologists for nonlinguistic culture. They are subject to much the same difficulties as the latter: arbitrariness of scale, indefiniteness of boundaries, and the related problem of marginal entities. To illustrate the problem of scale we may, for example, posit a European-Northern Asian language area of vast extent, or we may, in a finer-grained classification, distinguish smaller areas, such as the Balkans. The number of such levels is arbitrary as compared with that of the definite levels of branching that characterize genetic classification. Again, since we are dealing with similarities that are attributable to language contact, a language may well share certain features that have arisen in this fashion with one group of languages in one direction and with another group of languages in another direction. Boundaries between groups may therefore be arbitrary, so that the simultaneous assignment to different areal groups involves no contradiction. Here again, areal classification lacks the definiteness that is inherent in the genetic model.

The third major type of classification, the *typological,* is still further removed from the genetic model than the areal, in that it is in principle ahistorical; the relevant criteria for classifications that are historically and nonhistorically based are very nearly mutually exclusive. For this reason, differences between the assignment of languages in genetic and typological classifications are not only noncontradictory; they are, in fact, to be expected.

The difference between genetic and typological procedures is a fundamental one, in that even the notions of resemblance and comparison employed are different. Let us consider first the criteria of similarity that are inherent in genetic comparison. Here the decisive instances involve the existence of external cognates—that is, of word forms that continue the original form from the ancestral language, but with differential modifications of sound and meaning over time. Thus the Germanic languages are distinguished as a genetic group because of the existence of such external cognates as English *bone;* German *Bein* (leg); Dutch *been* (bone, leg); Swedish *ben* (bone, leg), and so forth, all of which continue in modified form a presumed Proto-Germanic *bain* (bone, more particularly, leg). Two things are to be noted about such evidence: They involve resemblances in respect to both sound and meaning simultaneously, and these resemblances themselves are evaluated as such in terms of possible connections by historical processes of change. It is true, of course, that we have here phonetic similarity in the initial and final consonants of all the forms that is so great that, in spite of some differences, they are all indicated by the same letter in the orthographies of the languages cited. In fact, there are phonetic differences—for example, the initial Danish *b* is phonetically [ḅ], an unvoiced sound, whereas the English, German, and Dutch initial consonants are voiced.[2] The vowel or diphthong, of course, shows greater variation. What is significant is not, however, that on the basis of some static classification, all the vowels fall into some definable class, but that all of them are possible outcomes as the result of possible changes from a single original. Since sound change is normally the result of the alteration of single features at a time, sounds that correspond to each other in cognates are also normally similar when they are classified statically. This is of enormous heuristic importance in the actual classification of languages. Nevertheless, there are certain changes that are well-attested historically, in which the earlier and later sounds would have little in common on a descriptive basis —for example, *s > h*. Because this is an attested process of change, however, we shall regard Latin *sex* (six), English *six*, and Classical Greek *hex* (six) as "similar" in sound, from the point of view of dynamic comparison.

Not all genetically connected traits of related languages involve external cognates with dynamic sound-meaning similarities. If, in a number of related languages, for example, it is a common rule of word order that the qualifying adjective always precedes the noun, we may reconstruct this rule for the ancestral language. Thus, the existence of this common feature in the existing languages receives a genetic interpretation, even though it does not involve specific sound-meaning combinations. On the other hand, since only two possible basic orders are involved—that is, either the adjective precedes the noun or it follows it—the possibility that languages will agree in this matter without the resemblances being the result of common retention of an earlier trait is quite considerable. Hence, such conclusions are reached by the systematic comparison of related languages, only after some relationship has already been established by form-meaning resemblances that have been evaluated in terms of process.

Typological classification rests on statically defined resemblances and, characteristically, on those either of sound or of meaning, taken in isolation. Instances of commonly employed typological classification will illustrate this. For example, languages are sometimes classified as either tonal or nontonal. The criterion of tonality is the possession of sets of phonemes that are differentiated solely by pitch level or pitch contour differences. If we employ this definition, then every language in the world can be classified as either tonal or nontonal. The characteristic that is utilized as a criterion is evidently that of sound only, in isolation from meaning, since we are not concerned with the meanings of the specific word forms. The indifference of this procedure to historical considerations is shown by the fact that languages of the tonal type are found in a number of geographically disconnected and remote world areas—for example, Africa, Southeast Asia, and aboriginal Mexico. From all the available evidence, these are historically independent occurrences. On the other hand, even fairly closely related languages may belong to different typological classifications. Thus Swahili, which is nontonal, is genetically a Bantu language; as far as present knowledge goes, all the other languages in that family are tonal. Such discrepancies between genetic and typological results are found because tonality is far from being an historically stable characteristic: nontonal languages may become tonal, and vice versa.

The assumption that languages can be genetically classified in a valid way by such criteria depends upon an unjustified assumption of stability. If tonality were absolutely stable, then all the tonal languages of the world would have their origins in one or more protolanguages that were themselves tonal, and all the nontonal languages would have originated from one or more distinct protolanguages that were nontonal. In that case, no tonal language would ever be related to a nontonal language and, since this would also apply to protolanguages, the monogenetic theory of language origin for human language as a whole would be refuted.

An example of a semantic criterion is nominal sex gender. Here, once again, languages are classified typologically into two classes: those that have sex gender and those that do not. It is evident that a differentiation of languages on this basis will cut across genetic lines; for the same reason, sex gender languages may lose gender and non-sex gender languages acquire it. For example, if the languages of Europe were to be classified on this basis, English would go with the Finno-Ugric languages—Finnish, Estonian and Hungarian—and be separated from Dutch and German.

The two typologies thus far considered are of a particularly simple kind, in that each has involved only a single criterion of a yes-no type, so that there are only two logically possible classes of languages: those that possess the quality (e.g., tonality, sex gender) and those that do not.

Typologies may also assume greater complexity—that is, they may produce a larger number of logically possible classes of languages—in either or both of two ways: by diversifying the possibilities under a single criterion, or by employing a number of different criteria simultaneously. To illustrate the first of these ways, one could classify languages with regard to tone, but not merely into the two basic groups of tonal and nontonal. Since every tonal language must have a definite number of tonal phonemes, and in every case two or more, we could divide tonal languages into those with two phonemes of tone, three phonemes of tone, and so on. Further, we may distinguish level tones, during the production of which there is no perceptible change of pitch, from contour tones, which rise or fall. This allows us to construct several additional typologies—for example, one based on the number of tones and one based on the presence or absence of levels or contours, respectively.

Another way in which typologies can take on added complexity is through the use of comparative in place of categorical criteria. Suppose, for example, it were possible to develop a method by which it could be stated, given any two languages, which of the two was the more complex grammatically. In this situation, to be sure, we would no longer have a classification of languages, but rather the assignment of each to a position in a continuum.

Such comparative concepts can be given greater exactitude by the introduction of a metric—that is, by some function that would assign a number to each language. Classes could then be reintroduced by definitional decisions to place in the same typological class all languages whose values for this function were within certain mathematical limits.

These possibilities can be illustrated by reference to one aspect of a typology of language that was popular in the nineteenth century. Languages were at that time classified as either analytic or synthetic. An analytic language was one in which grammatical categories were typically expressed by individual words; a synthetic language, one in which grammatical categories were incorporated within the word as inflections. Thus, the English construction *I shall go*, in which first person singular subject (future) and the concrete verbal meaning are each expressed by separate words, would be regarded as analytic, by contrast with the Latin translation equivalent *ībō* (I shall go), in which the root *ī* (to go) and *bō*, the future first person singular inflection, are contained in the same word.

When certain American Indian languages were discovered—for example, Aztec—in which certain concepts, notably the noun object of a verb and the verb itself, were expressed as parts of the same word, so that concepts that were expressed by separate words even in a synthetic language like Latin were incorporated into the same word, the term *polysynthetic* was invented, to designate this still higher degree of synthesis.

The nineteenth-century procedure was thus categorical, in that each language was assigned to one of three classes—analytic, synthetic, or polysynthetic—although in accordance with somewhat vaguely defined criteria.

Sapir, in his discussion of the nineteenth-century typology, regards degree of synthesis as a kind of sliding scale.

In his tables of typological classification, which incorporate a number of criteria, he uses such terms as "very synthetic" and "mildly analytic," but still in a quite impressionistic way.[3]

The present writer has suggested a metric in place of the qualitative procedures employed earlier.[4] Since a language is all the more synthetic to the extent that it incorporates more meaningful units in its individual words, if we could regard the notions of morpheme and of word as being well-defined, we could arrive at a measure of overall complexity by dividing the number of morphemes by the number of words over samples of text. Since, by definition, every word must presumably have at least one morpheme, the lower logical limit for this ratio is 1; a language with that value for the morpheme-word ratio would represent the logical extreme of analyticity. Among the counts made thus far, the highest value encountered is 3.72 for Eskimo, which is traditionally considered to be a polysynthetic language. If we define the values 1 to 2.2 as analytic, 2.2 to 3.00 as synthetic, and higher than 3.00 as polysynthetic, the assignments thus arrived at will probably correspond quite well with earlier intuitive judgments.

It was mentioned earlier that a typology can be rendered more complex by the simultaneous application of several criteria. An example in point is a proposed typology of word order, involving three sets of criteria. The first of these is the customary relative order of noun-subject, noun-object, and verb in the main clauses of declarative sentences. If we symbolize these as S, O, and V, respectively, then we have six possible orders and thus six possible classes of languages: VSO, VOS, SVO, OVS, SOV, and OSV. English, for example, would belong to the third of these, the SVO class. A second criterion is the existence of preposition as contrasted with postposition. English is an example of a prepositional language, since it has constructions of the type *in the house,* or *after dinner,* in which the relational concept is expressed before the nominal concept. There are many languages, however—for example, Turkish—in which the opposite order is customary, as in Turkish *ev-de* (house-in). The third criterion is the order of the possessor and the possessed in the genitive construction. A few languages, such as English, have two constructions—for example, *the house of the man* and *the man's house.* Putting aside for the moment this complication, the simultaneous use of the three criteria just referred to—the first with six possibilities, the second with two, and the third with two—will produce 6 × 2 × 2 or 24 typological classes.

The arbitrariness of typological, as compared with genetic, classification should be evident from this exposition. There are as many classifications as there are criteria capable of being used. Even with essentially the same criterion, the finer-grained the specifications, the larger the number of typological classes. Since, by definition, historical significance is disclaimed, it is natural and justifiable to raise the question of the purpose of typological classification. As will be shown in detail in the next chapter, the basic contribution that can be made by typologies is as a heuristic device in formulating generalizations about human language.

In general, zero membership or a proportionately small membership of languages in one or more of the classes defined by a typology leads to unrestricted universals or conditional generalizations about language. What seem with the usual type of statement to be merely tendencies often become susceptible to lawlike generalizing statements when the task of constructing a typology is undertaken, and the nonexistence of languages of certain logically possible types is revealed. For example, the tendency has often been noted of final obstruent consonants to be unvoiced.[5] Thus, in German, only unvoiced obstruents occur in word final; yet, since there are languages, such as English, in which voiced obstruents (e.g., d, v, z) do occur finally, no universal formulation seems possible. Nevertheless, if we construct a typology with two criteria, each of a yes-no type—the presence or absence of voiced obstruents in word final, and the presence or absence of unvoiced obstruents in word final—thus producing $2 \times 2 = 4$ typological classes, it becomes clear that one type appears to have no occurrences. There is apparently no language that has voiced obstruents but no unvoiced obstruents, while the other three classes do have members: (1) both voiced and unvoiced (e.g., English, French); (2) unvoiced, but no voiced (German, Russian); (3) neither unvoiced nor voiced (Mandarin Chinese, Hawaiian). From this there follows the universal implicational statement that, if any language has final voiced obstruents, it also possesses final unvoiced obstruents, but not necessarily vice versa.

An incidental value of typological classification is that it requires the development of definitions and procedures that can be applied to all languages, so that in every case it is possible to state that a language either does or does not belong to a particular typological class—that is, does or does not give definite results in regard to the application of the criteria employed in the typology. It therefore sets up a strong condition of universal applicability on all the linguistic concepts that are utilized in the construction of typologies. Nevertheless, as will be shown in a later discussion, not all universals have corresponding typologies, while, in certain instances, although typologies exist, they do not provide the most expeditious method for arriving at linguistic generalizations.

A further related application of typological analysis is in the study of the more comprehensive aspects of change in related languages. The procedures of comparative-historical linguistics are designed to account for specific and detailed similarities in related languages by processual changes from a common original. It is not, however, equipped to deal either with such questions as the extent of common directions of change in related languages that have developed from a common base, but in historical independence of one another (the so-called *problem of drift*), or with the related problems concerning the invariant as against the contingent characteristics in the evolution of such languages. Here we are dealing essentially with the degree and type of change over time of typological characteristics. Hence the typological comparison of individual languages in a single family at different historical periods can help in the establishment of overall trends. For example, in Indo-European languages, the general trend has been toward the simplification, in some cases (e.g., French) the loss, of case systems in the noun. What is involved is change of type from the class of languages that have case systems to the class of those that do not. Such general factors are sometimes discussed, of course, by comparatists; in so doing, however, they are moving out of the traditional framework, so that it would seem to be of some value to make such problems explicit and to pursue them systematically by the use of typological and related methods.

It will have been noted that typology as here described is purely synchronic: Languages are classified typologically by means of criteria that are applicable to synchronic language states. If, however, we do not confine the notion of classification in linguistics to synchronic states, then diachronic processes, such as those that were discussed in the last chapter, also involve what are essentially typological criteria. The language changes that are classified under the same process are of potential occurrence everywhere and at all times, as well as in historically independent cases. But, of course, the unitary items that are assigned to the same typological classes are the specific changes rather than the languages themselves. Just as synchronic typologies are of value in arriving at synchronic generalizations about language, so, as will appear later, diachronic processual classifications can assist in the formulations of universals of change.

The three approaches to language classification outlined here—the genetic, the areal, and the typological—are the ones that have been most important in linguistic practice. They are not, however, the only methods of classifying languages; some principle of language classification is implied in certain other commonly used terms regarding language that are encountered in the linguistic literature. In contradistinction to the three methods already discussed, however, these involve criteria of a historical or sociolinguistic nature that are, strictly speaking, external to language. Expressions such as *literary language, standard language,* and *pidgin language* suggest the possibility of additional classifications—for example, into languages that exist in written form and those that do not. It was suggested earlier that the popular conception of the distinction between language and dialect was basically of this nature. Such a classification is obviously nonhistorical, in that the usual assignment of a language either to the class of the literary languages or to that of the nonliterary languages has no implications about its historical connections. Whether or not a language is written seems, at least to the professional linguist, a nonintrinsic fact about the language. When the relevance of such a classification for linguistics proper is considered, then the question at issue is, precisely, whether or not languages that are classified in this fashion show purely linguistic common characteristics such that they would be assigned to the same class, according to the internal linguistic criteria that are employed in some possible typology. If so, then the empirical correlation between the linguistically external fact of writing and the typologically internal facts of structure are of linguistic interest. For instance, it might be conjectured that various positively evaluated characteristics that are attributed to literary languages by literary specialists—normally without rigorous demonstration, although some of them are probably susceptible of objective investigation—may have a basis in fact. One possible example is the semantic feature of richness in quasi-synonymity, along with the careful drawing of semantic distinctions among items with similar meanings. If such be the case, then the external criterion is correlated with legitimate internal typological criteria.

Pidgins and creoles are likewise characterized by external criteria of a sociolinguistic and historic nature. A *pidgin* is a drastically modified form of some language, used as a purely auxiliary form of speech and without serving as the first or exclusive language for any population. When a language of this type does become the first language of a population, it is usually called a *creole*—for example, Haitian Creole, which is a creolized form of French, and the Krio of Freetown, which has an English basis. Here again, the question at issue, one that has been, in fact, widely discussed in the literature on pidgins and creoles, is whether or not languages that originate in the specified fashion have certain linguistic—that is, typological—characteristics that distinguish them from other languages. The criteria suggested have usually been those of morphological simplicity, vocabulary limitations, and a relative lack of phonological fixity. These are, of course, qualities that tend to evoke negative reactions, just as the characteristics that are generally attributed to literary languages lead to positive evaluation. This suggests that a scaling of languages, on the purely external fact of valuational and other attitude scales (for example, potency), would provide a unified framework. In addition to the obviously nonlinguistic implications of such studies for intergroup attitudes, political language policy, and educational planning, they are also relevant to the study of language contact and language change, insofar as prestige ratings by speakers, of their own language and other languages with which they are acquainted, are factors in determining the extent and type of interlinguistic influence.

A possible classification whose basis as external or internal requires further investigation is the following. It has often been noted that languages meet the requirement of developing a new terminology in response to cultural and environmental change by characteristically different proportional uses of four basic methods. These are: (1) new combinations of internally existing resources by derivation or compounding; (2) imitation of foreign patterns by way of internal resources, as in German *Wolkenkratzer*, a literal translation of English *skyscraper;* (3) direct borrowing from foreign languages; and (4) the semantic extension of existing words (for example, when such terms as *captain, steward,* and *embark* are extended in English from sea travel to air travel). Are the varying predilections of different languages in this regard (for example, English borrowing, in contrast to the German use of indigenous compounds and derivatives), a consequence of structural linguistic facts in the language concerned, or are they a reflection of a non-linguistic cultural set of values? If the former, there is a significant relation between a typology embodying these structural facts and the changes undergone in a contact situation.

The truly basic importance of internal typological classification for linguistic studies is thus enhanced rather than diminished by the consideration of various classifications that are based on external criteria, since certain important questions concerning the relation of language to sociolinguistic, cultural, and historical conditions can be most clearly stated as involving an inquiry into the congruence between such external criteria and the linguistic internal criteria that are employed in typological studies.

# VIII

## SYNCHRONIC UNIVERSALS

In considering the conditions for adequate descriptions of individual languages, we set as a fundamental requirement that the methods be in principle applicable to all languages and that the resulting descriptive statements be of such a nature as to maintain the possibility of interlinguistic comparison. This basic commensurability of categories was seen as making possible the classification of languages in terms of their resemblances and differences. Yet classification is only a means to an end, a preliminary step on the way to the formulation of general statements about all human language. Our discussion of one type of classification, the typological, made a case for this when it was pointed out that a basic purpose of typology was to systematize sets of interrelated criteria in such a way that generalizations about human language would become possible. It was also shown that such generalizations will often be conditional or implicational—that is, they will take the following form: given that a language possesses a predicate $\alpha$, it will always possess $\beta$, but the converse is not necessarily true. That is, given possession of $\beta$, a language need not have $\alpha$. Our purpose in the present chapter will be to pursue in greater detail the topic of synchronic linguistic universals—that is, to consider what types of linguistic statement can be made that will hold true for all languages, when we compare the results of synchronic descriptions.

In this connection, it will be of fundamental importance to draw a distinction between two types of generalizing statements about language. In the first of these types, we assert the existence of a limited set of universal categories in terms of which certain specific aspects of all languages can be described. One example of this is the current theory of binary distinctive features in phonology, in which the claim is made that all distinctive sound oppositions in all languages can be adequately accounted for by positive or negative specification for each of a very limited set of features, approximately twelve. (Just so although somewhat more doubtfully, in view of the lack of adequate cross-linguistic definitions and procedures, it would have been asserted by the advocates of the traditional *grammaire générale* that the classification of words into the traditional parts of speech— noun, adjective, verb, adverb, preposition—provided a universal framework adequate for the assignment of any word in any language to one of these sets.) Generalizations of this type, which will here be called *categorizing*, have in a sense already been considered in our earlier discussion of the requirements for an adequate theory of linguistic description, since in that context no principle of categorization was regarded as adequate unless it was in principle applicable to all languages.

This requirement is not as severe in practice as it may seem to be in the statement of it. Sometimes rather different descriptive theories may all be adequate to the task of stating such categorizing universals. Thus, both binary theory and what may be called *traditional phonetics,* which makes use of certain sets of categories for defining sounds chiefly on an articulatory basis, seem to be adequate to the task of assigning all human speech sounds to one of a limited number of types. Such rival theories may, of course, differ in various other respects—for example, economy—which leads us to prefer one to another. For the moment, however, the criterion that will be relevant to our purpose will be relative usefulness in the discovery and formulation of cross-linguistic generalizations.

Some of the most basic formal generalizations may be regarded as being constitutive of language itself. They involve categories of so fundamental a nature that we might regard them as possible definitional characteristics of language, so that their absence would warrant our excluding the system under consideration from the set of languages. Among the examples of such characteristics are the existence of recursive mechanisms for producing an infinity of messages, and the distinction between phonological and grammatical level. In general, those qualities of human language that were discussed in the first chapter as distinguishing it from other types of communication may be considered to be potentially definitional. The empirical claim is, then, that all human communities have the institution of language—that is, one or more systems that possess these definitional characteristics.

The other type of universal, the one that will chiefly concern us in this chapter, is the sentential. We may illustrate the distinction between categorizing and sentential universals by reference once again to the theory of distinctive features in phonology. The categorizing universal is represented in the claim that the theory provides an adequate classification for the assignment of all sounds in all languages. Viewed purely as formal theory, however, it makes no existence claims as to which of the possible combinations are in fact found in some languages and which, if any, are found in all languages. In addition, however, the theory as usually propounded does make some substantive claims—for example, that the vocalic and consonantal features are universal, or, stated more precisely, that every language contains some nonempty class of phonetic segments with the feature of consonantality and some such class with the feature of vocality.

Such sentential universals may be called unrestricted, by distinction from the conditional or implicational type referred to earlier, in that these universals apply to all languages in unconditional fashion. The logical form of such a universal would be $(x)x \in L \rightarrow \phi(x)$—that is, for all values of x, if x is a language, then x has the predicate $\phi$. Thus, in the above example, if we assign to the variable $\phi$ the meaning "possessing the vocalic feature," then our unrestricted sentential universal will be statable in this form. On the other hand, if we wish to state an implicational universal—for example, that any language that has a dual inflectional category has a plural inflectional category, but not necessarily vice versa—then we shall obviously require a more complex statement involving two predicates, say $\phi$ and $\psi$, which will take the following logical form: $(x) \ x \in L \rightarrow (\phi(x) \rightarrow \psi(x))$. That is, for all values of x, if x is a language, then, if it has the predicate $\phi$, it also has the predicate $\psi$. In the present example, $\phi$ will be the property of having the dual, and $\psi$ that of having the plural, as an inflectional category.

It was noted in the previous chapter that every such implicational universal that involves two properties has an associated typology, in which one of the logically possible types has no existing language as an exemplification. To illustrate once more from the above instance, we may classify languages on the two criteria of the presence or absence of a dual inflectional category ($\phi$ and not-$\phi$, respectively), and correspondingly for the plural ($\psi$ indicates the presence of plurality and not-$\psi$ its absence). Then the four possible classes of languages are: (1) $\sim \phi. \sim \psi$, neither dual nor plural (e.g., Chinese); (2) $\phi. \sim \psi$, dual absent but plural present (e.g., English); (3) $\phi.\psi$, both dual and plural present (e.g., Classical Greek); and (4) $\sim \phi.\psi$ dual but no plural (no examples). The nonexistence of members of the fourth typological class of languages, which has a dual but no plural, is evidently logically equivalent to the implicational universal that, if a language has the dual, it will always have the plural.

The unrestricted universal, which at first sight might seem to be the only justifiable type, can now be shown to be the mathematically limiting case of a typology that is based on a single predicate. Thus, if we assert as an unrestricted universal that all languages have vowels, then there is the implicit associated typology that is constructed from a single predicate $\phi$, the property of having vowels. There are two typological classes, that of languages that have the property $\phi$ and that of languages that do not. The second class is empty, since there are no languages that do not have the property of possessing vowels. This parallels the earlier result with two predicates and four logically definable classes of languages, of which one is empty; this led to the formulation of an implicational universal.

We conclude that there is a reasonable basis for including implicational universals as valid generalizations about language. Further, one can point to the fact that scientific generalizations as a rule hold only under certain stated conditions, even in such advanced sciences as physics—for example, within certain limits of pressure.

Indeed, conditional generalizations are, for a number of reasons, of strategic importance in the study of the general properties of human languages. They are far more numerous than unrestricted generalizations, they exhibit interrelationships among linguistic variables (for example, the dual and the plural), and they establish hierarchical relations among linguistic categories. For example, the fact that the dual implies the plural—that is, that the former cannot exist without the latter being present—while the converse does not hold, permits us to conclude that in some sense the plural is a more fundamental category in human language than the dual. Most importantly, as will appear, such generalizations can often be shown to exhibit interconnections with each other, to form a structure, at least in some instances, a system in their own right, that leads to the formulation of higher-level generalizations of which the individual implications then become examples.

Once we have broadened the logical bases for generalizations about language, so as to include the implicational type that involves the relation of two predicates, there seems to be no reason for confining universals to the unrestricted and conditional types. The natural formulation appears to be that we will regard as a legitimate universal any statement that has as its logical scope the set of all natural languages. In terms of the symbolism employed earlier, this means that all statements are accepted that are of the type $(x) \in L \ldots$ (for all values of x, if x is a language, then $\ldots$).

Among the additional types that become acceptable on this liberalized basis are some that we may call *statistical*— that is, instances in which a particular relationship holds with considerably more than chance probability, in terms of some acceptable confidence limits. These have been called *near-universals* in that, in most instances, they arise from unrestricted or restricted nonstatistical universals, to which one or a very small number of exceptions has been found. For example, among the classes of sounds that are found in virtually all languages are nasal consonants. A small group of American Indian languages of the Northwestern part of the United States (e.g., Quileute) have been discovered, however, that do not have these sounds. Such a near-universal involves a generalization about language; it is a statement about a nonchance phenomenon that requires theoretical explanation that may show significant connections with other general facts about language.

Such near-universals may also be implicational. For example, it is generally true that a distinction of sex in the second person singular pronoun implies its presence as well in the third person, but not vice versa. There are a small number of languages in Nigeria, however, for which this apparently does not hold, in that they have second person singular masculine and feminine pronouns, but only a single pronoun in the third person, which designates a person of either sex. If we think in terms of the associated typology, then, in such examples as these, one of the cells, instead of containing a zero value, as in the nonstatistical universals, has a very small nonzero value. Evidently such cases can be treated by chi-square or other standard statistical measures.

In doing so, however, we are confronted with a problem that is fundamental to all applications of statistical methods in crosscultural comparison—namely, what is to be considered a single independent case. In most of the cases that we encounter in linguistics, this difficulty is in the nature of a quibble: the number of exceptions is usually so small that the distribution remains statistically significant.

Nevertheless, statistical universals are certainly less satisfactory than the nonstatistical variety, and not only because of the technical difficulty just discussed. The exceptions are themselves phenomena that call for explanation. It is, therefore, preferable not to be satisfied with a mere statistical predominance, however impressive it may be, but to investigate other factors in the exceptional cases in order, if possible, to reformulate the generalization in a more complex but nonstatistical form—that is, to account for the exceptions by some additional factor.

Other important classes of universals are those that rest on frequency distributions, in which the units are languages themselves. Such distributions arise whenever numerical predicates are assigned to languages. If, for example, the number of phonological units (phonemes) can be specified for any language by a method that is applicable crosslinguistically, then the distribution of languages with respect to that number of units can be plotted, and the various statistical measures of central tendency, dispersion, limits, and so forth, that pertain to this distribution can be regarded as universal facts about language—for example, that the number of phonemes in the various languages of the world have an approximate lower limit of 10, an upper limit of 70, and a mean of about 35.

Not every quantitative measure of language need be treated in this fashion. In fact, it is often not the intuitively reasonable procedure. For example, where nouns are inflected for two numbers, singular and plural, the evidence thus far shows a consistently greater *text frequency* for the singular. The property of having a greater text frequency for singular than for plural, in accordance with some generally accepted statistical standard of significance, can be regarded as a categorical predicate, which a language either does or does not possess, and a universal can be stated without having to have recourse to a frequency distribution over languages. This is also true for statements about limits of particular kinds—for example, that no language has more than five phonemic pitch levels. Here it is possible to have either categorical universals, like the one just stated, or to consider the number of languages that have tonal systems of two, three, four, or five levels.

Whenever they are dealt with in terms of frequency distribution, and in certain other cases (e.g., those of numerical limits), metrical characteristics may be called *inevitable universals*. By an inevitable universal we mean a universal that is an answer to a question that inevitably has an answer, provided the terms employed are operationally adequate. For example, there must be a largest number of tonal levels that can appear in a language; there must be a mean for the number of phonemes for a language. In such cases, if additional evidence refutes the generalization as hitherto formulated, it also produces, by its very refutation, a new generalization to take the place of the former one. Thus, if a language were to be discovered that has six phonemic tone levels, we would replace the old universal that stated five to be the maximum with a new one that establishes six as the limit. On the other hand, if, to turn back to an earlier example of a noninevitable universal, we found a language with an inflectional dual but without a plural, our universal that dual implies plural would be simply replaced, or would rather become a statistical universal. For this reason, inevitable universals are in themselves less noteworthy than non-inevitable ones. They become significant only if they can be predicted from other considerations—if, for example, some theoretical reason can be adduced to show that no language should have less than ten phonemes.

The work thus far accomplished in the area of synchronic universals indicates that a very considerable number of statements (several hundred) can be made, to which few or no exceptions have been discovered up to now, and which therefore take the form of unrestricted or, as is more often the case, implicational universals. Most of these are among the reasonably well-defined aspects of language, such as the structure of phonological systems, types of sound sequences, morphological categories, word order, and the semantic organization of certain aspects of vocabulary—for example, number and kinship systems. The remainder of this chapter is devoted to the examination of a sample of such universals, selected with a view to exhibiting the main logical types, and to a consideration of the chief aspects of the linguistic structures to which they refer. These samples are also designed to provide a specific background in terms of which the problems of deductive connections among generalizations can be dealt with in a preliminary fashion, in anticipation of the more systematic treatment of this topic, which is reserved for subsequent chapters.

We consider first some generalizations that may be made in regard to the phonological structure of language. A large and important subset of these is constituted by those that involve hierarchical relations among phonetic features. Typically, we find a number of separately statable universals, all of which involve some relation of superordinate and subordinate between the same features.

As our first example, let us consider the status of oral and nasal vowels. Phonetically, oral vowels are those in which the velic is raised, so that the entrance to the nasal cavity is closed and the air escapes only by way of the mouth. In a nasal vowel, the velic is kept down, so that air is expelled through both the mouth and the nose. If the other features of the articulation—of these the most important are the tongue position and the absence or presence of lip rounding—are constant, then two vowels may differ solely in regard to the contrast between orality and nasality. English, for example, has no nasal vowels; French, on the other hand, is a well-known example of a language with nasal vowels.

The subordinate status of nasal vowels can be shown in a number of ways. We may begin with a typology that involves two simultaneous categorical criteria, the presence or absence of oral vowels and the presence or absence of nasal vowels, giving four logically possible typological classes of languages: (1) those with both oral and nasal vowels; (2) those without nasal vowels; (3) those without oral vowels; and (4) those with neither nasal nor oral vowels.

However, there are no languages without oral vowels; this gives us an unrestricted universal. On the other hand, there are languages without nasal vowels. We can thus state an implicational universal—namely, that the existence of nasal vowels in a language implies the existence of oral vowels, but not vice versa. We can readily see that in such implicational statements the implied term—in this case the oral vowel—is all the more fundamental since the implying term (nasal) may not exist without the implied (oral), while the implied (oral) may exist (as in English) without the implying term (nasal).

A still stronger statement is possible. There are, indeed, a fair number of languages in which the number of nasal vowels and oral vowels is the same, but there are also many instances, as in French, in which the number of nasal vowel phonemes is less than the number of oral vowels. What seems never to occur (at least, no case of this has ever been cited), is a language in which the number of nasal vowels is larger than the number of oral vowels. We can, therefore, state as an unrestricted universal that, in every language of the world, the number of oral vowels is either equal to or greater than the number of nasal vowels. For those languages without nasal vowels, this will also hold since, in these instances, we can say that the number of nasal vowels is zero.

It might be thought that, since we have included the absence of nasal vowels as a special case, in which their number is zero, our second statement is sufficient and includes the first. The fact is that they cover the same ground only in part, as can be shown by hypothetical situations that would violate the first of our generalizations but not the second, and vice versa. Thus, the existence of a language with six nasal vowels and five oral vowels would violate the second of our generalizations, but not the first. If there were no languages in the world without nasal vowels, the second generalization would not be violated as long as the nasal vowels were never greater in number. While the first generalization would not, strictly speaking, be contravened, however, it would lose its raison d'être. Nasal vowels would still imply oral vowels, but oral vowels would also now imply nasal vowels; the implication would be mutual, and the hierarchical relation destroyed.

We can go still further by considering the text frequency of the vowels. As far as can be seen from a still admittedly small number of investigations, the overall frequency of nasal vowels is always smaller—in fact, usually far smaller—than that of oral vowels. The results thus far available are set forth in Table 2.[1]

In this case, the logical independence of the results from the previous universals is even more obvious, since it is possible for there to be an equal or smaller number of nasal vowels, yet for their text frequency to be greater, which seems, in fact, never to occur. An even stronger statement is generally possible. Where, as is most often the case, there is an oral vowel that corresponds to every nasal vowel, for each particular pair the frequency of the nasal vowel is smaller than that of its oral partner. There is, however, at least one exception. In French, according to Valdman's data, the frequency of $\tilde{o}$ is greater than that of its nonnasal counterpart $o$.[2]

TABLE 2

|  | Oral | Nasal |
|---|---|---|
| Bengali | 98.1 | 01.9 |
| Chiricahua | 92.6 | 07.4 |
| French | 82.5 | 17.5 |
| Mundu | 81.6 | 18.4 |
| Portuguese | 86.0 | 14.0 |
| Ticuna | 89.0 | 11.0 |

We can summarize our results thus far by indicating that a number of universals can be stated about the relationship between oral and nasal vowels, which are logically independent, either wholly or in part; all of them point to the relatively more fundamental status that is to be assigned to oral than to nasal vowels in human speech.

The example of oral and nasal vowels is far from being an isolated one. There are other sets of phonetic features for which a number of linguistic generalizations can be established; these lead in each case to the positing in a similar fashion of an underlying hierarchical relationship. As a further example, we may consider the relationship between consonants that are produced with the simultaneous closure of the glottis (so-called glottalized consonants) and their nonglottalized counterparts. While glottalized consonants are not found in European languages, they are common elsewhere—for example, in American Indian languages, in the Caucasus and in Ethiopia. A number of generalizations can be made about the relationship between glottalized and nonglottalized consonants that parallel those about nasal and oral vowels; in them, the nonglottalized consonants appear to be basic, in relation to the glottalized ones. Thus, the presence of glottalized consonants implies the presence of nonglottalized consonants, but not vice versa. In fact, all languages have some nonglottalized consonants, just as all have some oral vowels. The number of glottalized consonant phonemes is never larger than the number of nonglottalized ones, and the total text frequency of nonglottalized consonants, in all cases thus far investigated, is substantially greater than the frequency of glottalized consonants. Again, with a few exceptions, this holds for every pair that consists of a glottalized consonant and its nonglottalized partner.

Relationships similar to those just described for the nasal/oral contrast in vowels and for the glottalized/nonglottalized contrast in consonants hold for a number of other features.

A still higher degree of generality is possible, however, if we consider the articulatory and acoustic nature of the less and the more basic sound feature for each pair. The less basic feature always turns out to be more complex, in some objectively specifiable manner. Thus nasal vowels have a resonance chamber, the nasal cavity, in addition to the oral cavity that is involved in the production of oral vowels. A glottalized consonant involves the closure of the glottis as an additional articulation in its production. In Prague terminology, the more complex features are called *marked*, the simpler ones, *unmarked*. We thus begin to adumbrate a generalization about the more basic status of less complex articulations. Moreover, the procedure employed here is proof against the usual charge of circularity made against theories stated in terms of ease, that is, theories in which it is asserted that certain alternatives are favored over others because they are easier. Such putative circularity may be stated as follows. "Easier alternatives are favored. We know they are easier because in fact they are favored." In the procedure described here, however, certain objective relations among sound features are investigated, without any use being made of presumed simplicity or complexity. It is then found that the basic feature in each of these relationships is more complex, in some objectively formulable manner that is based on physiological and acoustic factors, independent of the earlier inductively developed generalizations.

The terms *marked* and *unmarked* have also been applied to grammatical categories. This terminology is justifiable insofar as, in a roughly similar way, hierarchical relationships of an equally far-reaching nature are found to obtain there. As an example, we take the category of number in its most common form: the distinction between singular and plural. Whether in noun, pronoun, adjective, or verb, the singular always appears to be the basic or unmarked member, and the plural the marked or nonbasic one. This relationship appears in a number of ways. The text frequency of the singular is always substantially greater than that of the plural. Where other grammatical categories, such as gender and case, coexist with that of number, the plural almost always shows less or equal differentiation with regard to the interacting category or categories. For example, in Russian, adjectives are distinguished by three genders— masculine, feminine, and neuter—in the singular, but by only a single set of forms, undifferentiated for gender, in the plural. In Latin, two cases, the dative and the ablative, are always identical in form in the plural, while being in general distinct in the singular. Again, it is typical of the unmarked category that it has no overt mark. Thus, in English, the singular of the noun is normally signaled by a mere zero, while the plural, except for a few irregularities, is indicated by one of the three variants /s/, /z/, or /ɪz/ (orthographically -s or -es). Where a zero is not involved, it is customary to find greater irregularity in the unmarked member of the category. For example, in German nouns, all dative plurals uniformly have -n or -en, depending on purely mechanical phonological factors, whereas the dative singular varies both with gender and with declensional class.

A common semantic characteristic of the marked category may be called *facultative expression.* One example is the expression of plurality in the noun by the suffix *-tul* in Korean. It need not always be used. Thus, the form that is labeled singular in Korean grammars, which has zero expression, may be either singular in interpretation or, on other occasions, plural. It would perhaps be more accurate to say that the form that is commonly called "singular" stands ambiguously either for the singular member of the opposition or for the category singular/plural as a whole, while the "plural" can stand only for the plural. Just so, to cite a lexical rather than a grammatical example, in English *man,* the *unmarked* member of the contrasting pair *man/ woman* stands either for *man* = human being, the category that contains both male or female, or *man* = male human being, whereas *woman,* the *marked* member, can designate only a female.

The hierarchical relation of marked to unmarked is merely one of a number of very general principles of this kind, each of which underlies a whole series of concrete universals. To refer once more to phonology, there are certain characteristics concerning the manner of organization of physiological-acoustic continua, of which the most striking is certainly the tendency to binary polarization which has been made the basis of phonological theory by the binary school. Typically, when such a continuum is given, of all the theoretically possible divisions, that into two terms is by far the most common, and the two physical extremes, rather than the intermediate points, are chosen as realizations. For example, although varying degrees of lip rounding are possible, all of which produce acoustically distinguishable stimuli, no language is known to use more than two degrees distinctively: the extremes of rounded and unrounded. Again, while vowels can be prolonged so as to produce a considerable number of degrees of vowel length, no language has been found with more than the two degrees of contrastive duration.

On the other hand, where the range of distinguishable effects is greater—as for the height of the tongue or for level pitches in vowels—three distinctive qualities are extremely common and tend toward an optimal spacing that consists of the two extremes and an approximate midpoint. Thus, no language with three degrees of vowel height will have, say, high, mid-high and mid, thus using only one end of the continuum, but rather, as a general rule, high, mid, and low.

Another principle concerning the division of continua is more relevant to grammatical and semantic categorization: in general, we have an avoidance of discontinuity. The following will serve as an illustration. No language in its treatment of number has, for example, a system in which sets with one or three members belong to one category, while those with two, four, or more members belong to the second category. The most common systems are one/two or more, one/two/three or more, and, far more rarely, one/two/three/four or more and one/two/three/four/five or more.

A similar principle may be seen at work in the semantics of kinship terminology. A by now traditional typology of such terminologies classifies systems on the basis of their designations for close male relatives of the first ascending generation. The kin types involved are the following: father, father's brother, mother's brother. There are five logically possible types of such kinship terminology. If we symbolize the kin types just referred to by the letters A, B, and C, then there is one type in which a single term designates all three; there are three types in which there are two terms—one designating A, B, or C, as the case may be, and the other covering the two remaining kin types; finally, there is one type with three terms, in which A, B, and C are each named by a separate kin term. The first type, in which there is a single term for father, father's brother, and mother's brother, is called *generational*, while the type in which one term indicates a *father*, and the other both father's and mother's

ical, and the typological, which is synchronic and
ng. This view coincides largely with the widely
otomy of history and science that goes back to the
-century German philosophical tradition, as found
itings of such men as Windelband and Rickert.[1]
iew of diachronic linguistics as particularizing has
been supported by the preemptive use of the term
ve for specific genetic reconstruction and specific
histories. This is natural enough, since these al-
olve comparisons of the results of synchronic
has therefore seemed that, while diachronics also
mparative method, it leads only to the discovery
c historical events, by contrast with synchronic
l comparison, which aims toward the establish-
eneral laws.

conception has been supported by the notion of a
aration between the diachronic and synchronic
f linguistics, the heart of the influential doctrine
ssure, who was the forerunner of modern struc-
In calling attention to the autonomous value of
c pursuits and the existence of systematic struc-
ions on a single time plane, de Saussure performed
service. If any one view has been held in common
verse schools of structuralism that came to dom-
uistics in the post-Saussurean period, it is the value
rtance of intralinguistic synchronic relations. In
riumph was so complete that, by contrast with the
in the nineteenth century, diachronic linguistics,
still an admired activity, has ceased to hold the
the theoretical stage.

s natural enough, then, that when linguists began
nce again to the problems of language universals,
ld do so chiefly in the synchronic idiom to which
grown accustomed during the intervening period.
attempt here will not be so much to refute this
oy the use of general arguments, as to show by
examples how diachronic generalizations may be

brother, is called *lineal*. Our system belongs to this latter
type, since it distinguishes *father* as lineal only from *uncle*
as collateral. The type that uses one term for father and
father's brother and a second for mother's brother is extremely common; it is called *bifurcate merging*. A type is
also to be found in which three separate terms are used for
A, B, and C (*bifurcate collateral*).

One logically possible system never found, however, is
the one in which one term is used for the father and the
mother's brother and a second term for the father's brother.
That such a system would involve a kind of logical disjunction or discontinuity can be seen by examining the
common characteristic that may either unite or divide the
various kin types. Thus we may divide them as lineal
(father) versus collateral (father's brother, mother's
brother), in which case the nonoccurring system would
unite the lineal with just one of the two collaterals and
thus cut across this principle. A second division, based on
unilineal affiliations, would group father and father's brother
in the paternal descent line, as against the mother's brother
as a maternal relative. Our hypothetical system also cuts
across this classification. Indeed, there is no characteristic
based on relation by blood or marriage that would allow
us to classify the father with the mother's brother, while
excluding the father's brother.[3]

From these and other similar examples, we can see
that individual synchronic universals are in many instances
not isolated but part of more comprehensive structures,
even if, at present, we are in only the initial stages of their
specification. Granted the existence of these broader principles, since language is a dynamic phenomenon, it will
follow that limitations on structure imply limitations on
the kinds of changes that systems must undergo. Whatever
else may happen during the course of historical development, there are certain invariants—namely, the universal
properties of languages—that must be maintained during
the course of change. Hence, there must be principles of

diachronic process, just as there are principles of static coexistence, and the two sets must be interrelated. Indeed, the fact that the synchronic question is usually raised first results in all probability from the by now deeply ingrained habits engendered by a half-century of structuralism. We might just as logically regard processual regularities as primary and their static results as predictable outcomes. In fact, as the next chapter will demonstrate, there are individual instances in which the approach in which process is primary, and the regularities of state derived therefrom, seems natural and intuitively preferable.

# DIACHRONIC

In the the possibilities of developin principles about language b synchronic descriptions; we problems in the field of lan the specific instances of cha direct historical method and of classical genetic linguisti universe comparable to the single languages in synchro as historically unrelated sync the subject of generalizing a independent instances of pro ilar changes.

In taking this approach, counter to certain common studies. Corresponding to the tion—genetic and typological types of comparison: the ge

and histor
generalizi
held dich
nineteenth
in the wr
The
probably
*comparat*
language
ready in
studies. It
has its co
of specifi
typologica
ment of g
This
strict sep
aspects o
of de Sau
turalism.
synchroni
tural rela
a needed
by the di
inate ling
and imp
fact, the
situation
although
center of
It w
to turn o
they shou
they had
The
position
concrete

attained and, more importantly, how diachronic and synchronic principles are in many instances intimately connected, so that one sheds light on the other. It is thus not a question of assigning priority to one or the other, but of investigating their interrelationships.

It might seem that a certain priority should be assigned to synchronic studies, insofar as diachronic conclusions can be drawn only from the comparison of descriptions that have been already made by the synchronic method. This is true as far as it goes, but it does not take into account the fact that the notion of a purely synchronic description is itself an ideal fiction, of a kind that is no doubt highly useful, indeed, indispensable in scientific investigation, but whose ideal character should be recognized. Thus, we have seen in the earlier discussion of phonology, that the free variation of sounds, such as $s$ and $h$, which do not form an exclusive class from the viewpoint of synchronic classification, may intrude into synchronic description and that an indication of the direction of ongoing change is a basic datum within a dynamically organized synchronic description.

In what follows, the isolation of certain among the possible types of diachronic universals will be incidental to the consideration of diachronic-synchronic relationships and will start from further considerations that arise in connection with the type of synchronic generalizations that were treated in the previous chapter.

There it was seen that hierarchical implicational relationships in phonology may be derived by way of typologies in which one or more of the logically possible types is found to lack empirical exemplification. Thus, to turn back to the first topic treated there, the relationship of nasal to oral vowels, it was found that only two of the four logically possible types of languages, which were specified by the presence or absence of oral or nasal vowels respectively, are actually found—namely, one type with oral vowels only, which we shall call type A, and another with both oral and nasal vowels, which will be designated as type B.

As we pointed out in discussing the distinction between typological and genetic criteria, typologically similar languages may arise repeatedly and in historically independent cases, while, on the other hand, related languages, during the course of changing from a genetically uniform basis, may change typologically in different ways. From this it follows that there should be instances in which, either by the direct historical or by the genetic comparative method, we can follow the change from type A to type B, and vice versa. As a general case, we may say that, for every typology with single or multiple criteria, it is possible to raise the question of change between any two existent types and in either direction. We may thus associate with every typology a state-process diagram, as shown in the accompanying figure, which illustrates the particularly simple case of the relationship of types with reference to the presence or absence of oral or nasal vowels.

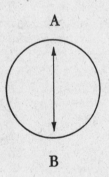

Figure 3

Since we have seen that oral vowels are basic, in that they are present in all languages and are thus implied by the presence of nasal vowels, we may think of the latter as an added feature. This leads one to restate the question in the following form: By what process or processes do languages that have only oral vowels acquire nasal vowels (i.e., how do languages change from type A to type B)? A theory that provided the answer to this kind of question would then be called a *theory of relative origin,* since it indicates how nasal vowels arise independently in different times and places. Correspondingly, we might ask how languages that have both nasal and oral vowels tend to lose the former and so to change back from type B to type A. This method of putting the question in terms of the relative origin and disappearance of nasal vowels does justice to our intuition that, since oral vowels are found in all languages, we do not need a diachronic theory to account for their existence in any given case, while for nasal vowels, whose existence in any language is a contingent one, such a theory does make sense.

Note that, when we ask the question about the relative origin of nasal vowels, in order to answer it we must compare the results of specific historical and genetic comparative studies that are themselves independent of one another, i.e., from different language families and different chronological periods. In other words, methodologically we move to a wider form of comparison, in which the individual cases that figure in the comparison are themselves the result of the historical-comparative method, applied in the traditional, narrower sense of the term.

A provisionally satisfactory theory of the origin of nasal vowels has, in fact, already been propounded as a universal by Ferguson in the following form: "Nasal vowels, apart from borrowings and analogical formations, always result from the loss of a primary nasal consonant." [2]

There is implicit here a typical sequence of events, of which the loss of the nasal consonant is the last and decisive happening that gives phonemic status to the nasal vowel. To begin with, in a language with only oral vowels, these vowels sometimes develop nasal allophones when a nasal consonant either precedes or follows. Since almost every language in the world has nasal consonants and since the sequences CV and VC are universal, nearly all languages have sequences of the types NV and VN (where N stands for nasal consonant). If the nonphonemic—that is, predictable—nasalization in the sequences NV or VN or in both takes place, we then have NṼ, ṼN, or both (where Ṽ stands for nasalized vowel); when it is not adjacent to a nasal consonant, V is still oral. If thereafter the event specified by Ferguson occurs—namely, loss of the nasal consonant in these environments—the nasal and oral vowels are now in direct contrast. For example, if the case involves VN, then in the first stage a sequence such as *$ant$ becomes *$ãnt$ while *$at$ remains. In the second stage $n$ is lost so that *$ãnt$ > *$ãt$, which now contrasts directly with *$at$.

A theory of relative origin, such as the one just sketched, may be regarded as the diachronic analogue of synchronic implicational universals. Instead of there being two characteristics in the same synchronic state, however, the implying characteristic will be one of a given language at some particular time, while the implied characteristic will be one of the same language at an earlier period. Put more formally $(\phi)L_{t_1} \rightarrow (\psi)L_{t_2}$ where $t_2$ is earlier than $t_1$. In the present example, $\phi$ will be the property of having nasal vowel phonemes and $\psi$ the property of having nasalized allophones that are conditional on the presence of nasal consonants. Actually, more is required than this, but it is not conveniently statable in existing logical symbolisms. We do not postulate merely that, in an earlier state of the language, nasalized allophones existed under the stated condition, but also that there are internal cognates in which later nasalized vowel phonemes are the historical continuation of earlier nasalized allophones. Since a generalized statement of this kind is, as we have seen, a statement of regular sound change, what is here asserted is the prior occurrence of a sound change, or rather a sequence of such changes: (1)

development of nasal allophones; (2) loss of nasal consonants.

For synchronic universals, the implied term is the basic one. For the corresponding diachronic universals, the implied term is a property of the earlier state of the language. This accords with our intuition that, in historical processes, earlier events explain later ones, and not the other way round.

In advancing a theory of relative origin, we have to recognize the limitations in the scope of what is asserted. Thus, nothing is said about the time interval between $t_1$ and $t_2$, nor is it claimed that a language without nasal allophones will eventually develop them, or that, if it develops them, they will eventually become phonemic. In other words, there is no element of predictability. What is asserted is that, wherever we find nasalized vowels in a language, they have come into being by a sequence of two changes of the type described earlier.

The relation between the diachronic universal just stated and the set of synchronic generalizations concerning oral and nasal vowels can now be considered. It appears that some of these synchronic generalizations can be logically deduced by arguments in which diachronic universals figure (although not exclusively), in the premises.

It has been noted that the text frequency of nasal vowels is always less than that of oral vowels. Take the case of the origin of nasalized vowels from sequences of the type VN (the same argument will hold, with appropriate changes, for the other types). If nasalized vowels arise from earlier sequences of vowel and nasal consonant, then, after the changes have occurred, the total frequency of nasal vowels should parallel the earlier relative frequency with which oral vowels are followed by nasal consonants, as compared with those in which oral vowels are not followed by nasal consonants. That this should hold seems to be a priori plausible as a synchronic generalization. If we assume that other fluctuations—the results of obsolescences, new vocabulary items, and morphological analogy—exert a random effect, then the synchronic universal about the greater text frequency of oral vowels will be deducible from the diachronic-origin theory, in conjunction with the synchronic-frequency hypothesis about the greater frequency of vowels that are not followed by nasals as compared with those that are.

Latin and French[3] offer a good test of this theory since Latin vowels followed by nasals are the historical predecessors of French nasalized vowels: In Classical Latin, the frequency of vowels followed by nasals in the same syllable is 14.7 as compared with 85.3 for vowels not followed by nasals; in French, the relative frequency of nasal vowels is 17.5 and of oral vowels, 82.5.

Diachronic considerations will also help in deducing the synchronic universal that nasal vowel phonemes are never greater in number than oral vowel phonemes. We again use the example of origin from sequences of type VN. Usually, the set of vowels that occurs with a nasal consonant following is identical with the set of vowels that occurs in all other environments. When this holds, then, at the time they originate, every nasal vowel will be matched by a corresponding oral vowel that differs only in nasality; the two will therefore be equal in number.

There do not seem to be any languages with a greater variety of vowels before nasal consonants than in other environments. If this observation is correct, then when nasal vowels arise, they can be the same in number as oral vowels, or fewer, but never more. To this we may add a further diachronic fact—namely, that merger seems to occur more often among nasal vowels than among oral vowels. We might propose here a diachronic universal to the effect that merger between any pair of oral vowels presupposes the previous merger of the corresponding pair of nasal vowels, where these correspond. For example, in contemporary Parisian French the nasal vowel œ̃ is merging with ɛ̃, while the corresponding oral vowels *œ* and *ɛ* continue to remain distinct. There thus appears to be a mechanism for decreasing the number of nasal vowels relative to that of oral vowels, but no corresponding mechanism that functions in the opposite direction. To summarize, the synchronic universal that the number of nasal vowels is never greater than the number of oral vowels is deduced from two diachronic universals: the origin theory of nasal vowels from sequences that contain nasal consonants, along with the preferential merger of nasal vowels, as well as one synchronic universal concerning the smaller or, at most, equal number of distinct vowels followed by nasals, as compared with the number of vowels in other environments.

It has already been noted that our assertion about the frequency of nasal and oral vowels had only statistical validity. While the frequency of a particular nasal vowel is almost always less than that of its oral partner, there are a few instances to the contrary. The possibility of such exceptions is deducible from the diachronic generalization about preferential merger. It is quite conceivable that when a number of nasal vowels merge, the resultant vowel, which has the total frequency of all its distinct predecessors, should exceed in frequency the corresponding oral vowel, whose frequency has not been increased by merger during the same period.

We have not yet considered the reverse process, by which a language of type B—that is, a language that possesses both oral and nasal vowels—changes to type A, a language without nasal vowels. Here the process seems to be simply loss of nasalization. If there is an oral vowel that corresponds to the nasal vowel in all features except nasality, then that is a case of coalescence. It may be stated as a diachronic universal that if nasal and oral vowels merge unconditionally, the result is always an oral vowel. In view of the fact that the nasal vowel is usually of low frequency, the number of meaningful forms distinguishable by the nasal-oral contrast in a specific case is likely to be small.

This is, as it was in the case of the merger of nasal vowels with other nasal vowels, plausibly a factor favoring merger. This thesis is generally called the *theory of functional yield*.[4] As will be shown later, however, there are always other factors at work—for example, the greater perceptual similarity of nasal vowels to each other than is true for oral vowels—which makes it difficult to arrive at an empirical evaluation of this theory.

The relationship of nasal to oral vowels was treated earlier as one example of the general synchronic principle of the relationship between marked and unmarked categories. Our diachronic results are also, at least tentatively, generalizable in terms of this same class of oppositions. Typically, the marked feature arises by an initially nonphonemic modification of an extensive class of sounds, to be called here the *base class*, adjacent to a specified single phoneme or to a more restricted class of phonemes, which we may call the *independent segmental form* of the marked feature. Thus, in the origin of nasalized vowels, the class of oral vowels constitutes the base, while the more restricted class of nasal consonants is the independent segmental form of the marked feature of nasality. Nasalized vowels come into being by incorporating the nasality feature of the independent segment (the nasal consonants) into the base, while the independent segment is itself lost in the process. Similarly, the opposition between the marked feature of palatalization and the unmarked one of nonpalatalization may come into being through the adjacency of a base class that consists of all the consonants or some subset of them, and the independent segment *j*. However, the independent segment need not always disappear. For example, in palatalization, the independent segment may be a front vowel *i*, which ultimately merges with another vowel, rather than being lost.

The opposite process of the loss of a marked feature by merger with the corresponding unmarked one is also generalizable from the case of nasal and oral vowels. Indeed, if the process ever occurred in the opposite direction so that, for example, the oral vowels all became nasal, a system would result that violated the synchronic universal on which the original notion of hierarchy was based—namely, that there are nasal vowels without oral vowels. We see, then, that synchronic and diachronic regularities must be related, since no process of change can ever give rise to a system that violates synchronic norms.

To return once again to the relation of oral to nasal vowels, it can be seen that the origin theory of nasal vowels by way of the nasalization of oral vowels in the environment of nasal consonants receives powerful support from a corresponding synchronic universal. There are a number of languages in different parts of the world in which there is allophonic alternation of oral and nasal vowels. In every such case, as far as is known, the condition for the appearance of the nasalized vowel allophone is an adjacent nasal consonant. In general, every posited type of historically conditioned sound change should be reflected in allophonic variation somewhere among the vast number of synchronically described languages. Hypotheses of exclusive origin would in effect be refuted by the presence of allophonic alternation that involved a conditioning factor incompatible with the theory.

The value of diachronic theory in explaining exceptions in the synchronic hierarchical relations of marked and unmarked features has already been illustrated by instances in which a particular nasal vowel is more frequent than its oral partner because it is the resultant of the merger of a number of previously distinct nasal vowels. Another example has to do with distinctive length in vowels. In general, where the vowel system involves two contrastive lengths, short and long, it is the long vowels that have the characteristics of the marked or subordinate feature. Thus, the total frequency of long vowels always appears to be less than that of short vowels, a relation that normally holds for each pair. Further, it may be plausibly argued that additional length is the consequence of a superadded feature, such as nasalization, glottalization, etc. Contrary to the generalizations that are possible in these other instances, however, it is not uncommon to find languages in which the long vocalic phonemes are more numerous than the short ones.

The difference here becomes understandable if we have recourse once again to diachronic theories of relative origin. There is a considerable variety of diachronic processes by which systems of contrasting vowel length may arise. Unlike the case of oral and nasal vowels, we do not have a theory of exclusive—that is, single—origin. For example, length may arise in a word prosodic system in which the stressed vowel is longer than the unstressed and subsequent changes make the length contrast phonemic. Again, the loss of certain consonants in syllable final may result in the occurrence of added length in the vowel that immediately preceded. The loss of intervocalic consonants may result in vowel sequences where they previously did not exist; these may be later consolidated into long vowels in a single syllable. This latter process is one that is particularly likely to result in more long vowels than short vowels. Consider the following simple model. In the first stage, there are three vowels $a$, $i$, $u$ with heterosyllabic vowel sequences and no length distinctions that have resulted from the previous loss of intervocalic consonants. In the second stage, as a result of contractions—$a + a > a$:, $i + i > i$:, $u + u > u$:, $a + i > e$:, $i + a > \varepsilon$:, $a + u > o$:, $u + a > \mathfrak{o}$:, $i + u > u$:, $u + i > \ddot{u}$:— we would have eight long vowels as against three short vowels. On the other hand, when length develops from the **loss** of a syllable-closing consonant, the situation parallels **more** closely that of nasal and oral vowels, and we may expect that, at least initially, the number of short and long vowel phonemes will be equal.

This suggests not only that differences in the types of universals that hold for marked and unmarked features can sometimes be explained by diachronic considerations, but also that, where there are several kinds of origins, the same typological class of languages will correspondingly show different associated characteristics. Thus, languages in which vowel length has arisen from original stressed vowels, from vowel contractions, or from loss of syllable final consonant may be expected to show systematic differences, leading to the establishment, on this basis, of synchronic subtypes.

A further type of complex comparison, involving both synchronic and diachronic factors, may be likened to the use of successive snapshots to produce the effects of a moving picture. In essence, as will be shown later, it is the same method as the dynamic interconnection of typologies illustrated earlier in the chapter. The difference is a pragmatic one. Instead of starting with synchronic universals already arrived at and associated with typologies, we begin by isolating a single type and study the properties that are associated with the typological defining factor. We choose, naturally enough, a contingent property of language, preferably one that occurs in a rather restricted number of instances, so that it provides a manageable corpus for investigation.

We can illustrate this method by a consideration of voiceless vowels. Like nasalized vowels, voiceless vowels occur in only a limited number of languages, whereas voiced vowels are found in every language. Unlike nasal vowels, however, voiceless vowels almost never attain phonemic status.[5] The following conclusions are based on an incomplete sample of 50 languages, among which American Indian languages predominate. They must, therefore, be considered quite tentative. These are the conclusions that emerge from an examination of this material: (1) Voiceless vowels tend to occur in utterance final, sometimes also in word final: Final is, in general, favored over nonfinal position; (2) Where vowel length exists, it is short vowels that tend to be voiceless rather than long vowels; (3) Where stress exists, it is unstressed vowels that tend to be unvoiced, rather than stressed vowels; (4) Vowels tend to be unvoiced when preceded and followed by unvoiced consonants, particularly by nonsonants (i.e., stops, fricatives, and affricates); and (5) Vowels of minimum aperture—for example, the "high" vowels *i* and *u*—tend to be unvoiced, in preference to low vowels, for example, *a*.

The following are examples of typical rules about voiceless vowels. In Campa, an Arawakan language of South America, which has four vowels *i, e, o, a*, only *i* occurs voiceless and only when it is final in the word where it occurs in free alternation with voiced *i*. In Totonac, which is spoken in Mexico and has short and long *a, i* and *u*, all the short vowels are voiceless in utterance final. In Hawaiian, all utterance final vowels are voiceless. In Oneida, an Iroquoian language, which has vowel length, all short vowels are unvoiced in utterance final.

From these and similar data, the following are among the universals that can be tentatively derived: (1) Long voiceless vowels imply short voiceless vowels; (2) Stressed voiceless vowels imply unstressed voiceless vowels; (3) Word final voiceless vowels imply utterance final voiceless vowels; (4) Voiceless vowels adjacent to voiced consonants imply voiceless vowels adjacent to voiceless consonants; and (5) Non-high voiceless vowels imply high voiceless vowels.

As a near-universal, we may add, it is almost always true that the presence of voiceless vowels in utterance medial implies their presence in utterance final. There are three exceptions—Chatino, Chontal, and Japanese—languages in which voiceless vowels are found in medial but not in final position. We shall return to Japanese later, since it is a particularly instructive example in this regard.

From the viewpoint of origins, there are two independent factors. The first is the tendency for vowels to become voiceless when they are in final position, particularly utterance final. When this occurs, it tends to exercise a stronger effect on vowels that are in one of a set of "weak" categories—for example, high (that is, of minimum aperture and therefore of less sonority), unstressed, short, nonnasalized, and so forth. This weakening in final position is the more frequent of the two origins. It is in turn to be connected with a widespread tendency for consonants to become unvoiced in utterance final and for pitch to drop, as well as with other evidences of articulatory weakening in final position.

The other and less common origin of voiceless vowels is for the vowel to be both preceded and followed by voiceless consonants. Here too it is the "weaker" type that is most affected: vowels of minimum aperture, unstressed vowels, and so forth. Where this is the only origin, vowels in pause cannot be affected, since the voicelessness, as we have seen, occurs in this case only when a voiceless consonant follows.

We may now transform the synchronic universals by translating them into a form of speech in which relative time is equated, as earlier, with the implied. For example, the third statement above, according to which voiceless vowels in word final imply voiceless vowels in utterance final, becomes the diachronic thesis that voiceless vowels start in utterance final and then spread to word final, presumably by analogical extension, within particular words, into utterance medial of the form of final voiceless vowel that occurs in utterance final. If, indeed, it could happen in the other direction, this process has nevertheless left no trace in any existing language. Suppose that this opposite was able to occur. Then there might be a language in which the process of spread from utterance medial but word final to utterance final had not yet been accomplished. Such a language, however, in which, synchronically, voiceless vowels occur in medial but not final does not seem to exist.

Corresponding to statements (1), (2), and (5) above, we will expect short, unstressed, high vowels to be affected first, or at least not later than the other type. Similarly, for the less frequent case of vowels that become voiceless when they are adjacent to consonants, we expect the process to start in the environment of voiceless consonants and to attack, in the first instance, vowels that belong to the weak categories already referred to.

If we now turn to the synchronic descriptions themselves, we shall often encounter evidence of ongoing sound change. Considering the usual format of phonological descriptions, this evidence will be of two main types: free variation and distribution within styles. When one sound replaces another in a particular environment, there is presumably a period during which both the old sound and the innovating sound occur freely, as alternatives. The relative frequency of the innovative forms presumably increases as the process of replacement advances. In regard to style, many descriptions give data in the no doubt somewhat oversimplified form of a *lento/allegro* dichotomy. *Lento* forms are those of slow, careful, more formal speech, and *allegro* those of more rapid, less careful, and more casual discourse. An examination of the literature suggests very strongly that in phonology at least, the *lento* form is the earlier form and the *allegro* the innovative, since this is the usual time sequence where there is written evidence of changes in language.

A very instructive example is the distribution of voiced and voiceless vowels, as described for Japanese by Bloch.[6] Japanese has five vowel phonemes: *a, e, i, o,* and *u.* The high vowels, *i* and *u,* which, as we have seen, are more susceptible to becoming voiceless, are described as having voiceless variants when they are both preceded and followed by certain voiceless consonants. Since the rule embraces almost all voiceless environments, it is more easily stated in terms of those environments in which voiceless *i* and *u* do not appear —namely, when the vowel is preceded by *ts, tš, s, š, f, x,* or *h* and followed by *ts, tš, t,* or *k.* Historically, and also from evidence within contemporary Japanese that will not be discussed here, it can be shown that *ts* is the variant of older *t* before *u, tš* of *t* before *i; š* of *s* before *i; f, x,* and *h* are likewise variants before particular vowels of former *\*f.* We can therefore summarize the above statement in the following manner: voiceless *i* and *u* do not occur, when the vowel is preceded by *\*t, \*s,* or *\*f* and followed by *\*t* or *k*. According to Bloch, every phrase containing I (voiceless *i*) "is paralleled especially in slow or careful speech by an otherwise identical phrase containing i instead." If we interpret "especially" as "more frequently" and identify slow or careful speech with *lento,* as described above, we may paraphrase as follows: High vowels have voiceless and voiced vowels, in free variation, in both *lento* and *allegro* styles, but the proportion of voiceless vowels is less in *lento* than it is in *allegro.*

For the low vowels, as we would expect, the environments in which voiceless vowels occur is much more restricted than it is for the high vowels—namely, when they are both preceded and followed by *p, t,* or *k.* Yet among these few environments are included some in which voiceless variants of the high vowels do *not* occur, as a comparison with the earlier statement will show—namely, when *\*t* precedes and *p, t,* or *k* follow. Viewed dynamically, however, this paradox is resolved by the observation that voiced vowels do not occur in this environment either. In other words, the reason why we do not find unvoiced *i* and *u* here is precisely that this is among the most susceptible environments and the process has already progressed further, in that the former unvoiced vowels have now been lost and make their appearance only in lengthened consonants. This is illustrated by direct historical evidence. Thus, whereas the voiceless form of the lower vowel *o* occurs between *t* and *k* in t*o*koro (strength), we also have *tš·kara,* which is known to derive historically from *\*tikara.* Thus the exception to the generally valid synchronic statement that any environment for a voiceless low vowel is also an environment for a voiceless high vowel, but not necessarily vice versa, receives a reasonable explanation when we show that the apparently exceptional environment is one in which the process has already been terminated and has been followed by the next stage (loss of vowel).

As to voiceless low vowels, it appears that they occur only in rapid speech and that even there they are less common than the voiced variants. We conclude that the unvoicing of high vowels is older, in that it has already advanced beyond the *allegro* style, in which it is now dominant, to the *lento*, in which it is not yet as frequent as it is in the *allegro*. On the other hand, the low vowels are still confined to the *lento* form and even in this style they are not yet as frequent as the voiced variants.

It was noted earlier that Japanese was, viewed synchronically, one of the exceptions to the generalization that if a language has voiceless vowels in word medial position, it also has them in word final. Here again it turns out that this holds precisely because the process has already gone much further in word final, so that the formerly voiceless vowels have been lost. The former sequences *ti, *tu, *si, and *su in word final have been replaced by long consonants tš·, ts·, š·, and s· respectively. Thus we have *arimas·* (is) (polite form) from earlier *arimasu*, presumably with a transitional stage in which final *u* was voiceless.[7]

We may illustrate these principles further by an example from the grammatical sphere that will, incidentally, introduce still another type of comparison, which involves both synchronic and diachronic moments. In the earlier discussion of marked and unmarked categories, it was noted that in morphology it was the singular that was unmarked, and not the plural. To this we may add here that the so-called direct cases—those of the subject (nominative) and object (accusative)—show the characteristics of an unmarked category when they are contrasted with oblique cases, such as the genitive, dative, and locative. We have seen, further, that where the marked-unmarked relation obtains in morphology, it often happens that the unmarked or dominant category has no mark (e.g., the singular of the noun in English), while in the marked category this almost never occurs. An exception to this principle that might be cited is that of the so-called hard (*nonpalatalized*) declension of feminine and neuter nouns in certain Slavic languages, in which an oblique case of the plural—namely, the genitive—has a zero. For example, in Russian, the feminine hard noun for *woman* is *žena* in the nominative singular, but *žen* in the genitive plural. The fact is that this would not be an exception to the principle stated elsewhere—namely, that the marked category should never have zero as the *sole* allomorph or variant. There are whole classes of nouns in Russian, including feminines and neuters, in which the genitive plural *has* an overt mark—for example, masculine in almost all instances (*city*, nom. sing. *górod*, gen. plural *garadóf*), feminines of former *i*-stem declension (*bone*, nom. sing. *kós't'*, gen. plural *kós't'ij*), and softer neuters (*sea*, nom. sing. *mór'e*, gen. plural *mar'éj*). Still, absence of marking in so many instances of a marked category calls for some explanation.

An investigation of the history of Slavonic shows that, during the earlier period of Church Slavonic, the genitive plural always had an overt ending. In the instance of nouns like *žena*, where literary Russian has genitive plural *žen*, Old Church Slavonic had *ženŭ*. By a regular sound change, the two short vowels of closest aperture *ĭ* and *ŭ* were already lost in the later stages of Old Church Slavonic, in word final and in certain word medial environments.

Thus, regular sound change, operating in apparent independence of the grammatical system, produced a zero in the genitive plural, where it had not existed before. It is significant that the same sound change also left the nominative and accusative singular of masculine nouns without an overt mark. Thus the word for *nose* was in earlier Church Slavonic *nosŭ* in both the nominative and accusative singular; later, by the loss of final *ŭ*, this became *nos*.

It is not so important to observe that the genitive plural once had an overt mark as it is to study the dynamics of what is virtually a laboratory situation. The same sound change left both the unmarked nominative accusative singular and the marked genitive plural without an ending. The

whole subsequent history of Slavonic in this matter illustrates how, in the former case, the zero ending has remained
stable. Thus, in no Slavonic language have words of the class
*nos* acquired a new ending by the analogical spread of other
alternants. On the other hand, throughout the history of
Slavonic, genitive plurals have received overt marks by the
analogical spread of other forms. In Sorbian, the original
genitive plural of masculine *u-stems* (O.C.S. *-ovŭ*), which
almost everywhere replaced the earlier zero form of the
main masculine hard declension, has spread to all nouns. In
many nonliterary dialects of Russian, this same (originally
masculine) *-of* has now spread to the hard feminines and
neuters, so that virtually all genitive plurals have an ending.
In literary Serbo-Croatian, an ending *-ā* of somewhat ob-
scure origin is now uniformly added to all nouns except the
feminine *i*-stems, which already had an overt ending inherited from the Old Church Slavonic period. Even where,
as in standard Russian, the process is not complete, we see
a tendency for the spread of endings from the remaining
declensions into the genitive plural, but no such tendency in
the nominative/accusative singular.

The comparative study that is involved in studying a
question of this kind takes place within a restricted genetic
group of languages, in this case Slavic. On the basis of synchronically derived universals, we state a hypothesis in apparently purely Slavic terms.

The following diachronic hypothesis, for example, can
be stated for Slavic with regard to zero and nonzero endings
for marked and unmarked categories in the noun. The *-a*
nominative singular ending of the *-a* stems (nearly all
feminine) will not spread to the original *-i* stems (also
nearly all feminine), which have a zero in the nominative
singular. However, a change in the other direction—that
is, replacement analogically of *-a* by zero—may occur in the
(unmarked) category of the nominative singular. There is
no instance in Slavic in which the *i*-stems follow the analogy
of the *a*-stems in the nominative singular. On the other hand,

in Czech and Slovak, the opposite analogy has occurred and the feminine -*a* stems have in some instances taken over the zero ending from the -*i* stems.

Other principles, besides the tendency to overt marking in marked and zero expression in unmarked categories, can be utilized for diachronic hypotheses. For example, the -*ov* genitive plural of the original masculine -*u* stems is more likely to be analogically acquired by a masculine declension than by a feminine or neuter one. The spread of -*ov* as a genitive plural ending to a feminine or neuter declension implies its previous spread to some masculine declension. This is also verified by data from the Slavic languages.

It was noted earlier that explanation in terms of analogy, as it is usually stated, is incomplete in that analogy may often have several possible models to follow, of which only one can actually occur. Such hypotheses as are suggested here provide a basis for predicting the direction of the change or the more probable occurrence among two possible models.

Although these hypotheses are stated in regard to Slavic, they are particular only in appearance. For example, if in any other group of languages we were to encounter a similar situation with regard to zero expression of any marked category, we could derive from it a specific set of hypotheses about the diachronic course of events within the particular language family.

We have seen, then, that diachronic process is susceptible of general formulation; that diachronic and synchronic regularities are often intimately related, and that, in some instances at least, what appear to be exceptions to otherwise widespread synchronic universals are actually expectable by-products of the underlying diachronic processes that produce the regularities.

# HIGHER-LEVEL EXPLANATIONS

The formulation of synchronic and diachronic regularities and their interconnections clearly relate to the most fundamental goals of linguistic science. That we are in merely the initial stages of this process cannot be too strongly emphasized. The hypotheses presented in the last two chapters are to be viewed as preliminary suggestions, the obvious inference being that they require both expansion and more rigorous testing in the light of the relevant empirical data.

We shall now consider how conclusions arrived at by these methods are to be viewed within the context of the overall strategy of linguistics as a scientific endeavor. The goals of the individual sciences have commonly been expressed in terms of such concepts as scientific explanation of the phenomena of the particular field and the construction of a body of theoretical principles, or, as they are sometimes called, "laws." These and related concepts have, of course, been the subject of longstanding discussion and controversy in traditional philosophy and in the more recent philosophy of science, often with inconclusive results. The stance taken here in these matters is that of a practicing scientist; it is not designed to contribute theoretically to the solution of these vexing questions. Some comfort can be taken from the fact that results that are universally recognized as being truly scientific have quite often been attained by scientists who have only minimal sophistication in such theoretical matters, and that the actual task of the philosophy of science has been to explicate the common features of such acknowledged results. It would be difficult indeed to discover a clear-cut case of a scientist attaining his goals by the application of "the scientific method," as it is described in philosophically oriented treatises on the subject. Still, on the positive side, it can be maintained that some general notions of the type that are generally regarded as pertaining to the overall goals of science are at least implicitly present as an ultimate standard for the scientist and help to guide his endeavors, even where these are relatively lacking in precise formulation.

One of these goals, as has already been mentioned, is explanation. A particular science seeks to explain the phenomena that come within its purview. The concept of scientific explanation, like so many others, is only a refinement of "common-sense" notions of everyday life. In the latter context, we often ask questions; sometimes, at least, we receive answers that we accept as explanations, in that they induce a kind of satisfaction, which shows itself in our refraining thereafter from asking the same question. They seem to be satisfactory by certain rough standards, as when I explain my absence from a social engagement by reference to an illness whose actual existence in this case can be checked in terms of certain types of generally accepted evidence. The notion of "scientific explanation" arises, it would seem, out of an attempt to formulate with greater rigor the criteria of acceptability for such answers as can be considered to render unnecessary further questioning along these same lines.

What seems to underlie the notion of explanation is an asymmetrical relation that obtains between two items: that which explains (the *explanans*) and that which is to be explained (the *explanandum*). The *explanans* must be more general, in that it can be referred to in other instances in order to explain other particular facts. Thus my particular absence from a social function is "explained" in terms of a principle that relates illnesses in general to absences in general. Viewed logically, it is the *explanans* that makes it possible for the questioner reasonably to cease pressing the same question.

The explanations traditionally furnished by historical linguistics are only one instance of the familiar class of historical explanations that are found in such other fields as geology, evolutionary biology, and history proper. For example, if our curiosity is aroused concerning the marginal type of English plural by internal vowel change—for example, *tooth/teeth, mouse/mice, man/men*—it is a satisfactory explanation to show that, historically speaking, each of these apparently diverse instances, as well as still others not cited here, is an individual manifestation of the same process. In the "prehistoric" period, a plural suffix *-i* was the conditioning factor for the modification of the vowel of the preceding syllable, which was "fronted" in anticipation of the front quality of the *-i* itself (the so-called umlaut). Hence, we have the development from earlier *\*tōþi, \*mūsi, \*manni* to *\*tȫþi, \*mǖsi, \*menni*, followed by the loss of the final *-i* and the unrounding of *ö* to *e* and *ü* to *i*, giving *tēþ, mīs, men* and ultimately modern English *teeth, mice,* and *men*. All these are regular changes, in the sense described earlier. Since the umlauting of a vowel when *-i* occurred in the next syllable was not contingent on the *-i* being a plural suffix, we can bring still other cases under the same general explanation—for example, the irregular comparative and superlative *elder* and *eldest,* as compared with the positive *old*.

It is true that, like children, whenever we are offered

an explanation, we may then proceed to frame a higher-level why-question, which asks for an explanation of the explanation. Why did certain sound changes occur rather than others? Why did these particular plurals survive, while others conformed to the analogically vigorous *-s* pattern? Why, indeed, was the *-s* pattern so much more expansive? And so on, with a host of questions. Nevertheless, the kind of historical narrative that was presented in the previous paragraph may be legitimately regarded as explanatory, in that we no longer ask questions about the specific case of *tooth/teeth*. The question has now been shifted to a higher level and has to do with the whole class of which *tooth/teeth* is an individual instance. Here, as always, explanation involves the bringing of a particular event or a class of events under a more inclusive class.

In descriptive linguistics, even grammatical rules of the conventional sort are explanatory of particular phenomena, but with the difference that general statements of this type refer exclusively to phenomena that are synchronous with the *explanandum,* rather than referring to the past. If, for example, a student who is just learning Turkish is told that the plural of *diş* (tooth) is *dişler* while that of *kuş* (bird) is *kuşlar,* he may ask why the first word forms its plural by adding *-ler* while the second does so by adding *-lar.*[1] He may then be told that any word whose final vowel is *-i* takes *-ler,* while one in which the final vowel is *-u* takes *-lar.* This may be considered an explanation, insofar as further interrogation has to do with classes of words that have *-i* or *-u* as their final vowel rather than with the individual forms *diş* and *kuş.* If he asks about these two classes, he may be given a still more general statement, in which *-i* is but a member of the class of vowels *i, e, ü* and *ö* that have the common feature of front articulation, all of which as final vowels take the plural in *-ler,* while, correspondingly, the set of back vowels *a, ı, u* and *o* has the *-lar* as plural suffix. If he asks why the front vowels take *-ler* while the back vowels take *-lar,* he may be given an even more generalized rule regarding formatives with alternating forms in *a* and *e,* such as the two suffixes of the future *-acak* and *-ecek.* Pressing still further, he will finally receive a full statement of the vowel harmony system of Turkish, which brings under a very small number of highly generalized statements involving sound features a very large number of variations in the forms of grammatical affixes in Turkish.

There are then successive levels of generalization and hence of explanatory efficacy among rules that may figure in grammatical descriptions. The rationale of traditional structuralism, which hardly if ever spoke in terms of explanation, was presumably that the relations subsumed under structural statements were a set of higher-level generalizations, indeed the highest attainable. The great contribution of contemporary transformation theory is that it explicitly, and with a large measure of success, seeks to incorporate whatever generalizations are possible within the grammar, in terms of a uniform model that is applicable in principle to all languages.

Not all explanations, however, satisfy an additional requirement that may be said to characterize what have often been called *laws* in discussions of scientific method. In the present context, I would call these *general principles.* In other words, not every generalization (potential explanation) is a general principle. The difference rests in the limiting conditions within which the generalization is asserted to be valid. Such conditions may themselves be general (for general principles), or particular, in that they include proper names, which involve in a basic way specific space and time coordinates. The traditional modes of linguistic explanation, both historical and descriptive, must be regarded as belonging to the latter class—that is, to those explanations that do not attain the status of general principles.

Indeed, the only kinds of linguistic statements to which the term *laws* has been commonly applied are historical statements, such as Grimm's Law and Verner's Law; in principle, these are statements of regular sound changes, of quite the same type as those cited above in explaining English irregular plurals, such as *teeth* and *mice*. For example, Grimm's Law states, among other things, that the earlier unvoiced stops of Indo-European (*p, t, k,* etc.) were under certain conditions replaced by the corresponding unvoiced fricatives during the period of separate development that led to Proto-Germanic. As is usually pointed out in manuals of historical linguistics, such "laws" hold only for a particular language and during a specified time period. Its limiting conditions therefore involve proper names. Thus, it would be a meaningless question to ask whether any languages are known to be exceptions to Grimm's Law, since the law is asserted to hold, not under generally statable conditions but only, so to speak, if the language is pre-Proto-Germanic. We can thus ask the question sensibly regarding only that language, and for the period of validity of the "law."

The same limitation would seem to hold, in principle, with regard to even the most generalized rules in an individual language description. Thus, if we ask under what conditions the precise rules of vowel harmony that govern Turkish are valid, the answer would have to be "if the language is Turkish" or, if there are related languages, such as Uzbek, in which the rules are precisely similar, then "the finite disjunction of the particulars, Turkish, or Uzbek, or. . . ."

The purpose here is not to argue about the relative applicability of the term *law* or *general principle*. There is a real and important difference between them, however, that is recognized terminologically. If the conditions of application of a generalization are presented by proper names, then, given a hitherto unknown example that is not specifically mentioned in the rule, there is no way of predicting whether or not the principle is applicable.

The synchronic and diachronic universals described earlier do have this property of generality of the limiting conditions. If a hitherto unknown language is reported, we can predict that it will have oral vowels, and that, if it has low voiceless vowels, it will have high voiceless vowels, or that, if it has gender distinctions in the plural, it will have them in the singular, and so on. If it has nasal vowels, we can assert that these arose from former sequences of oral vowels and nasal consonants; the new example may provide a further test of our thesis by the application of either the comparative or the direct historical method. In effect, our limiting conditions are solely that it be a language. In practice, this will never be a real problem, but for theoretical purposes we may refer to the initial discussion for certain defining characteristics of language that are of a completely general nature.

Each new case, as we have seen, will not only generate a prediction, but, if the limiting condition holds, will also provide a further empirical test of the hypothetical universal. If it violates the hypothesis, then one possibility is that that hypothesis will become merely statistical. Where it is possible, however, the exceptional case or cases should be examined more closely, in order to see whether or not the limiting conditions need to be stated in more complex, though still general fashion. In this respect, they are not in principle different from the more particular generalizations that hold under proper-name conditions. Thus Grimm's Law was believed at one time to have a considerable number of exceptions, but these were largely accounted for by a more complex formulation that took into account the original Indo-European pitch accent (Verner's Law).

As we have seen, explanations, whether or not they are general principles, involve a hierarchy of levels. The lower-level explanation itself falls, as a special case, under a more inclusive explanation. For general principles, at least, such higher-level statements often involve terms that are not properly linguistic, in that they are not part of the ordinary terminology of linguistics but seem instead to refer as much to certain aspects of nonlinguistic phenomena as to linguistic ones. They tend, indeed, to take us into the somewhat shadowy regions inhabited by such hybrids as psycholinguistics and sociolinguistics. Thus, the synchronic explanation for the alternation of certain suffixes in Turkish is in terms of a vowel harmony system, for whose description a purely linguistic terminology is used. Again, the explanation of irregular plurals in English by reference to certain linguistic changes, such as the fronting of vowels before an *-i* in the following syllables, would seem to involve a purely linguistic terminology. In this case, however, it is fairly common to say that the earlier vowel has been fronted "in anticipation" of the front vowel of the following syllable. Most linguists, however, have learned to eliminate such apparently superfluous terminology, which attributes to the speakers a psychological act of "anticipation," apparently without adding to the value of the explanation.

For some higher-level general principles, such non-linguistic references become practically unavoidable. For example, the highly general principle of phonology that relates to the division of phonetic continua, while it arose from purely linguistic data, seems to be of very general applicability in regard to human perception and motor performance. The formulation and testing of these higher-level general principles in their full generality places us squarely in the realm of psychoacoustics and physiological psychology. If we seek a higher-level explanation as to why certain continua—for example, vowel duration and lip rounding—are exclusively polar and binary, while others, such as vowel height and pitch levels, more often than not have an interposed middle term that is roughly equidistant from the two extremes, we inevitably raise questions that are basically of the type investigated by the classical psychophysical branch of psychology. We shall inquire about the number of perceptually distinguishable positions on the different continua, and the correlated problems concerning the motor adjustments that are required for their production.

Where diachronic rather than synchronic general principles are involved, the correlated psychological investigation may be concerned with the general conditions for dynamic changes of behavior. We have seen, for example, that an important premise in explaining why nasal vowels are never more numerous than oral vowels is the diachronic hypothesis that nasal vowels have a greater tendency to merge with each other than corresponding oral vowels. It seems reasonable therefore to seek for a wider context of explanation by reference to the diachronic tendency rather than to its synchronically predictable outcome. This does not mean that the diachronic hypothesis might not in its turn be investigated, either statically or dynamically. For example, we may consider the static proposition that two nasal vowels are more similar perceptually than their oral counterparts, or we can seek experimentally to induce changes in linguistic behavior. A conspicuous instance of the overall theoretical significance of a dynamic approach for the study of change arises from the contrast between *lento* and *allegro* styles for a whole series of sound changes in language. Here the effects of speeding up speech need to be observed systematically, and generalized theories need to be developed about the locus of errors, in terms of the physiological and higher-level processes involved. Nor should it be forgotten that the perceptual aspect is also involved in auditory feedback to the speaker, as well as in the typical mishearings that presumably occur when a listener is exposed to more rapid speech styles.

In other instances, a static approach appears to be more natural. This will be particularly true with regard to unrestricted universals, which, since they hold unconditionally for all language, are precisely the characteristics of language that remain invariant under change. Thus, a concentration on static qualities seems justified in a theoretical consideration of the "optimal sound types"—that is, of those classes of sounds and of sound oppositions that are the building blocks, as it were, of phonological systems—for example, voiced oral vowels, voiceless stops, the contrast of vowels and nonvowels, and, at the other extreme, those sounds that, though they are physically possible, either are not known to occur at all in sound systems or, if they do occur, never develop into autonomous phonemes. These two extremes should presumably be embraced in the same general theory, which would thus provide the physiological and acoustic basis for placing sounds on some scale of effectiveness. Even here, however, diachronic considerations are sometimes relevant. For example, if a sound is rare but not completely absent from human speech, then that fact is correlated with general diachronic principles both of genesis and of further development. The sound in question can arise only under severely limited conditions and tends in subsequent change to be either replaced or lost altogether. Voiceless vowels are a case in point. They occur in a relatively small proportion of the world's languages and almost never develop as autonomous members of a phonemic opposition to voiced vowels. This is doubtless connected with the general diachronic fact that the normal change-product of voiceless vowels is zero—that is, they are lost.

It is reasonable to expect that a physiological and psychological theory that is adequate to the explanation of purely linguistic higher-level generalizations will be of so broad a scope that linguistic phenomena will be only a special case, falling under a body of hypotheses that have relevance to nonlinguistic behavior as well. In practice, this need not mean the subordination of linguistics to psychology or to any other nonlinguistic discipline. It is conceivable, rather, that the combination of complexity and definiteness that is characteristic of linguistic phenomena will provide precisely the challenge necessary for the development of more sophisticated theories of organismic behavior. It does not seem to be inescapable that psychology will have to account painstakingly for more and more complex functions; the actual work in that direction may well be accomplished collaboratively, as well as individually by linguists and psychologists.

The emphasis so far on psychology as the source for the highest-level explanatory principles for linguistic generalizations has been due mainly to the fact that our examples have been drawn from phonology. This need not always be the case. For example, the general preference for continuities as against disjunctions, which we observed in the organization of kinship terminologies, may be expected to occur in other semantic spheres as well, and thus to constitute a fundamental principle of folk classification, lying within the province of anthropologists who are interested in problems of comparative cognition. The study of semantic change inevitably draws on nonlinguistic cultural factors— for example, in the study of changes in terminology within specific technological areas, in relation to the development of technology. Again, there are sociological variables, as we have seen, that enter into the study of language change— for example, when we investigate the differential spread of linguistic features within a speech community.

The search for higher-level general principles, such as involve disciplines other than linguistics, doubtless violates a widely held view about the autonomy of linguistics. This, in turn, would seem to be an instance, in linguistics, of the more general notion of discrete levels of phenomena, each autonomous and with laws that are couched only in terms of its own level. The violation of levels, by which concepts of a lower level are used to explain those of a higher level, is called *reductionism*. It seems not unfair, and is here done without polemical intent, to call such views dogmas. By *dogma* is here meant any general metatheoretical principle that guides research and theorizing. A principle of this sort has a useful side, in that it generally contributes to a clear delimitation of what is relevant. On the other hand, after having fulfilled a useful or even necessary function, it may tend to become restrictive at a later stage of the development of a science. Even when it is maintained with good reason, such a principle nevertheless becomes so deeply imbedded in the earlier training and subsequent research of professionals that it comes to be taken for granted. It is therefore in need of periodic reconsideration and re-statement. During the course of the present work, we have encountered three such generally held assumptions among linguists: the autonomy of linguistics, the distinction be-tween diachronic and synchronic studies, and the *langue/parole* dichotomy, in its various similar although not identi-cal guises (most recently, competence versus performance). Each of these was at some point violated in the search for general linguistic principles. Since the same basic principle is involved in each case of violation, the methodological issue involved will be discussed first, and then more detailed consideration will be given to each dogma, in regard to both its usefulness and its limitations.

What we are concerned with here is the relation be-tween two main types of theoretic activity: the development of conceptual schemes—that is, of sets of coherently related concepts, such as those of binary theory in phonology—and the formulation of interrelated laws, or, as we have pre-ferred to call them, general principles. To return to the earlier discussion about the distinction between categorical universals and sentential universals, we may connect the first of these with the notion of conceptual schemes, the latter with that of general principles. As to the former, we consider whether a given set of concepts is adequate for the description of the linguistic phenomena under con-sideration. For example, in phonetics, we ask whether all the sounds that are known to occur in languages can be defined by a particular set of concepts and their relations. As to the latter, we employ phonetic terminology in stating principles of universal scope about the phonological aspects of language.

Concepts, then, face in two directions, as it were. On the one hand, they enter into relations with other concepts in general terminological systems, regarding which it is reasonable to raise questions of adequacy in covering the data, consistency, and logical simplicity (for here, as elsewhere, entities are not to be multiplied without reason). On the other hand, these concepts occur in the formulation of general principles—in which case we recognize no predetermined barriers to the free devising and utilization of concepts, provided only that they are applied consistently.

There is in fact a very real danger that classificatory conceptual schemes may involve the premature abstraction of factors that are relevant for the establishment of hypotheses. When this is so, we should feel free to utilize the excluded datum where it exhibits connections with other data and therefore seems to be required for some more extensive formulation. An example may be cited from binary theory in phonology. Its overall strategy is to eliminate all predictable categories (redundancies) in individual language descriptions. This is a reasonable and important goal, which comes under the general scientific canon of the *economy of entities*. If a particular feature, for example, is always associated with another feature but not vice versa, the occurrence of the second can be predicted from the first. We have, in other words, an in-language implication. If, as in many languages, nasals occur only voiced and never unvoiced, whereas nonnasal consonants occur in both voiced and unvoiced categories, we may state that nasality implies voicing, but not vice versa. This carries with it the prediction that for any nasal segment the value to be assigned to it in respect to the voicing feature is predictably plus. But, since it is predictable, it can be eliminated. Hence, in the definition of nasal consonants, the column for voicing can be left unspecified, since voicing never distinguishes one nasal from another. The prevailing practice in such cases is to use zero as the entry.

By this abstraction, however, we have eliminated the phonetic information that the nasal segment is voiced rather than unvoiced. If we were then to take the definitional tables with their maximal elimination of redundancies as our objects of crosslinguistic comparison, we would have de-

stroyed the possibility of stating a significant generalization
—namely, that for any language the presence phonetically
of unvoiced nasals implies the presence of voiced nasals.[2]
On the basis of such tables alone, the languages of the world
would fall into two typological classes. In the first of these
—for example, Irish—voicing is relevant in segments with
the nasal feature, so that the definition of *m* would have a
plus entry in the column for voicing, while its unvoiced
counterpart *m̥* would have a minus. In the other class of
languages, for which the voicing feature is not relevant
phonologically, the corresponding columns would have zero.
What would be omitted is the information that, wherever
the voiced feature is predictable, it is phonetically voiced
rather than unvoiced, so that the data on which the implicational generalization stated above was based would not
appear. Moreover, the priority of voiced over unvoiced
nasals is a generalization that is connected with still others,
such as the priority of voiced vowels over unvoiced vowels
and voiced liquids over unvoiced liquids. This particular
generalization about nasals therefore figures integrally as
evidence for a phonetic principle of wide import.

The methodological principle that we are free to use
whatever conceptual apparatus is required for the statement
of general principles and their logical interconnections leads
us to violate terminological restrictions that have sometimes
been set up in accordance with each of the three dogmas
described earlier: the distinction between *langue* and *parole*,
the autonomy of linguistics, and the separation of synchronic
and diachronic studies. The first two of these are connected
insofar as a definition of linguistic system (*langue*) as
against what is not language is involved in both. They all
have methodological correlates, generally left implicit, but
still powerful in practice: that predicates of certain types—
for example, those pertaining to *parole*—cannot figure in
explanatory statements that have to do with language; that
diachronic predicates cannot be employed in explanatory
statements about synchronic linguistics, and vice versa; and

that nonlinguistic (for example, psychological or sociological) terms cannot be used in explaining linguistic phenomena.

As to *langue* and *parole*, the basis for drawing the distinction has been vague in the past, and has differed with different linguistic schools and chronological periods. It seems to be most strongly anchored in the *type-token* distinction; this seems to be due to the fact that, in various occurrences of the "same" sentence, there are differences that are linguistically irrelevant—that is, not part of the code. With this has gone the tendency to view the type as normative or as supraindividual. What is linguistically relevant in theory or in practice, however, is not always clear and has varied with differences in doctrinal approach. For instance, classical structuralist phonological theory has often regarded allophonic variation as being below the linguistic level and allophones as not being part of the linguistic system.[3] If, for example, the /t/ phoneme regularly has predictably heavy aspiration in English before a stressed vowel, then these and other allophonic variations of the /t/ phoneme are not part of the "structure" of English. What we have here is evidently two conflicting interpretations of the notion "linguistically relevant," which underlies the *langue/parole* distinction. According to one of these interpretations, since aspiration within certain limits is always present before stressed vowels, it is one of the constants in all sentences with stop before stressed vowels, and hence belongs to the type, however variously it is implemented in actually occurring tokens. On the other view, *linguistically relevant* means capable of distinguishing one sentence from another; since aspiration is predictable, obviously neither its presence nor its absence can serve to distinguish sentences.

Another possible source of divergence has to do with the question of frequency. On the basis of the type-token distinction, text frequency, which is a synonym for token frequency, is not a part of linguistic structure. Yet certain aspects of text frequency turn out to be characteristic of the language in that they show statistically insignificant variability from text to text or else they may vary within certain limits, yet remain significantly related to "styles"—for example, learned, casual, and so on.[4] Again, there may be certain aspects of performance that show consistency, yet—as in the case of allophones—do not serve to distinguish one message from another. One example is the incidence of hesitation pause in certain cases in English. In such prepositional phrases as *in the house* the tendency is to "run together" *in* and *the* and to pause before the nominal member, particularly if it is relatively unfamiliar—for example, a proper name. In my own speech, in rapid conversational style I have, in fact, a contracted form *in ə* for *in the*. This division *in the house* runs counter to accepted grammatical analysis, which divides the phrase into preposition *in* + noun phrase *the house*. In grammatical analysis, such a concept as noun phrase, of which *the house* is an example, is a virtually necessary construct based on intersentential relations. The pattern noun phrase with minor modifications appears with the same basic patterns of construction, but in a variety of positions in different classes of sentences—for example, as subject in *The house is burning*, or as object in *I build the house*. In performance, however, other relations may take over. In this case, it is possible to regard transitional frequency as a factor. Given *in*, the frequency of *the* as a follower is very high, whereas given *the*, the frequency of any particular noun, adjective or other alternative for the next position within the noun phrase is low.

In these and similar cases, what is primary is not so much a question of what is *langue* and what is *parole*, but whether aspects of language that on one or another showing have been excluded from the linguistic system can serve in explanatory hypotheses. For each type of case cited here, examples have been given in which it figures in the explanation of facts that on any view are parts of linguistic structure. Thus, phonological linguistic universals, such as the preference for nasal + voiced stop homorganic clusters over all other sequences of nasal followed by consonant, applies equally whether the variation in nasals is allophonic or phonemic. To consider one subcase, no language has such sequences as *nb*, in which the nasal and the following consonant have different points of articulation, unless it also has sequences in which they have the same point of articulation (e.g., *mb*). But on some phonemic analyses for some languages, since the point of articulation is predictably the same as that of the following consonant, it becomes phonemically irrelevant, so that if we talk only in terms of phonemic units and their relevant features, these facts will not be usable for comparative purposes.

The importance of the relatively constant frequency relations among certain grammatical categories was earlier shown to be part of a widespread network of systematic relationships, subsumed under the terminology "marked" and "unmarked" categories—for example, the relation of the singular, the unmarked and more frequent category, to the plural, as the less frequent and marked category.

The relationship between preposition and noun phrase described here for American English apparently obtained in some Romance and Germanic languages, since it led to contracted forms—for example, French masculine singular *au* for *à le* (to the), German dative, masculine singular *im* for *in dem* (in the).

The emphasis on the synchronic-diachronic distinction that first appears explicitly in the pioneer writings of de Saussure has served a number of highly useful functions. It is to be considered in part a reform in the direction of clarity of exposition. The nineteenth-century emphasis on earlier states as explanatory of later states of the same language often led to such an expository mixture of synchronic fact with diachronic explanation that the temporal locus of the facts themselves was obscured and the distinction between hypothetical explanations and observable facts destroyed. The other important facet was the emphasis on the coherence of synchronic organization, and on the possibility of studying it in its own right, in abstraction from the historical factors that produced it. Here again, the emphasis on historical explanation had often distorted the organized structure of later stages of a language by describing it in terms of categories that were derived from a previously existing structure.

The modern structuralist movement has been so successful that the uncritical priority of historical explanations and the failure to represent linguistic structures in terms of their synchronic organization can hardly be considered any longer a danger. While we ought to maintain these gains in conceptual clarity and in the understanding of languages as involving relationships among elements in the same time plane, it is also necessary and holds no threat to these accomplishments to study intensively the relationship between diachronic and synchronic phenomena. Such an approach has been sketched in a preliminary fashion earlier in this work.[5]

As with the *langue/parole* dichotomy, that of the autonomy of language, which rests on the definitional distinction between language and nonlanguage, has performed valuable services. It is the very importance and centrality of human language, and the variety of points of view from which it may be approached—for example, from literature, psychology, philosophy, social sciences—that has in the past led the linguist to seek for a delimitation of linguistics in terms of an interest in language as an end in itself, not (as with other disciplines), as a means, however important, to other ends. Here, as in the related case of *langue* and *parole*, the attempt to delimit language from nonlinguistic phenomena has not always been carried out in the same fashion. Thus the *meaning* relation, particularly in the case of lexical designation—for example, that the English word *table* designates "table," has seemed to some not to be part of linguistics, since it involves references to extralinguistic events. In this way, semantics has been excluded by some from linguistics, and language has been viewed as a calculus, concerned with the rules of permitted combinations of abstract items, divorced from their context of meaning. Others, also calling themselves structuralists, have not excluded meaning. Again, on the phonological side, the argument could be advanced that linguistics as a science was concerned only with the structural relations among units that had been abstracted from their phonetic content. Just as semantics required reference to nonlinguistic data, in the form of the extralinguistic designata, as part of the meaning relationship, so phonetics involved articulatory phenomena that pertained to physiology and acoustic facts that belonged to the acoustic branch of physics. In excluding the concrete data of both semantics and physiology, linguistics becomes the study of purely formal relationships abstracted from content. Although this point of view has been influential, it has never become dominant.

Here again, the motives that once led linguists to seek an autonomous and self-contained subject matter no longer obtain. Linguistics now has an indisputable place among the sciences, as well as a well-defined subject matter and methodology. It need not fear any longer that it will sell its linguistic birthright for a mess of psychological, sociological, or any other alien pottage. The autonomy of linguistics has performed a useful function in directing the attention of linguists to the search for linguistic variables, in order to account for linguistic phenomena, in the first instance, and to avoid a mere facile paraphrase of linguistic results in the terminology of other sciences. But the search for deductive explanations of universals that were themselves established on the basis of extensive linguistic observations, and within a context of interrelations with other linguistic variables, is a different matter. Here, as with the other distinctions that have tended to assume a dogmatic form, it is important to maintain the necessary freedom of maneuver and to make reference to variables, from whatever source, that appear to be required for explanatory theory.

The recent revolution in linguistics has reopened many

issues and produced an atmosphere that is favorable to the reformulation of old questions and the broaching of new ones. It has also stressed the universal aspects that underlie all organized language behavior. It is hoped that the lines of investigation sketched in this book will prove fruitful in developing a truly deductive edifice of general principles, embracing both static and dynamic aspects of language, as well as the connections between language and the social, psychological, and environmental matrix within which it perpetually functions.

# Notes

CHAPTER I. **THE NATURE AND DEFINITION OF LANGUAGE**

[1] *La filosofia è scritto in questo grandissimo libro che continuamente ci sta aperto innanzi a gli occhi (io dico l'universo), ma non si può intendere se prima non s'impara a intender la lingua, e conoscer i caratteri ne' quali è scritto. Egli è scritto in lingua matematica. . . . Le Opere di Galileo Galilei,* Vol. VI (Florence: Berbèra, 1933), p. 232.

[2] Reprinted in Carleton S. Coon, *Reader in General Anthropology* (New York: Holt, 1948), pp. 3–43. Gibbon cries are enumerated and described in the table on p. 32.

[3] See Karl von Frisch, *Bees: Their Vision, Chemical Senses, and Language* (Ithaca, N.Y.: Cornell University Press, 1950).

[4] I am indebted to discussion with Sol Saporta for this a fortiori proof.

[5] Another semantic property of natural language, which might be preferred by those who find various difficulties with the concept of translation, is the following. We can state the rules of bee communication in natural languages, but the bees cannot formulate the grammar of a natural language in their own system. Hence, natural languages serve as metalanguages for other communication systems. Parallel, then, to the distinction set forth in the text, we might say that natural languages are universal metalanguages and the only such metalanguages. That is, it is possible in any natural language to state the grammatical rules of any communication system, including that of the language itself and that of any other natural language.

[6] The marginal exceptions run here in both directions. Certain systematic aspects of sentence intonation—for example, sarcastic intonation—are not expressed in existing orthographies. On the other hand, there are some orthographic devices, such as quotation marks and capitalization of pronominal references to the Deity, that have no correspondence in spoken language.

## CHAPTER II. LINGUISTICS AS A SCIENCE

[1] Edward Sapir, *Language: An Introduction to the Study of Speech* (New York: Harcourt, Brace, 1921), p. 234.

[2] Ferdinand de Saussure, *Cours de linguistique générale* (Paris: Payot, 1916); English translation, *Course in General Linguistics* (New York: Philosophical Library, 1959).

## CHAPTER III. DESCRIPTIVE LINGUISTICS

[1] It would be a gross oversimplification to think of increase and decrease of frequency, in these and other cases considered here, as necessarily being gradual over time. A speaker who uses two variant forms might, after hearing some speaker with social prestige use one of the forms, quite suddenly adopt it as his exclusive form. An obsolescent form might on occasion be revived. Particularly in a literary language, there is always the possibility of the revival of a hitherto dormant form that has been preserved in the dictionary. Such a revival could perhaps be regarded as an innovation—for example, the reappearance of the virtually obsolete term *sibling* by social scientists in English.

## CHAPTER IV. GRAMMATICAL THEORY

[1] See particularly in this regard the attempts to integrate semantics into the overall grammar by members of the transformational school—for example, Jerrold J. Katz and Jerry A. Fodor, "The Structure of a Semantic Theory," *Language,* 39 (April–June 1963), 170–210; Jerrold J. Katz and Paul M. Postel, *An Integrated Theory of Linguistic Descriptions* (Cambridge, Mass.: M.I.T. Press, 1964), and the recent works of Uriel Weinreich, especially "Explorations in Semantic Theory" in Thomas A. Sebeok, ed., *Current Trends in Linguistics,* Vol. III (The Hague, Paris: Mouton, 1966).

[2] However, there was also a strong element of nominalistic "fictionalism" in the American linguistic approach of the period

under discussion—for example, in W. F. Twadell's classic monograph *On Defining the Phoneme* (Baltimore: Waverly Press, 1935). One is reminded of Boas' distrust of Western categories and his attempt to describe cultures in their own terms; he combined this with a deep skepticism about the possibility of devising any set of concepts that were not arbitrary inventions of the observer.

[3] Phonemic transcriptions are put between slant marks, phonetic transcriptions between brackets, and morphemes between braces.

[4] Charles C. Fries, *The Structure of English: An Introduction to the Construction of English Sentences* (New York: Harcourt, Brace, 1952).

[5] The classic example of this procedure is Zelig Harris, "From Morpheme to Utterance," *Language*, 22 (July–September 1946), 161–183.

[6] This device seems first to have been suggested by Leonard Bloomfield in *Language* (New York: Holt, 1933), p. 217 fn., where, for example, the masculine singular of the French adjective is derived from the feminine singular by means of minus-feature—namely, loss of the final consonant and of the cluster -*kt*. Given such pairs as /lɛ/ *laid* (ugly, m.s.); /lɛd/ *laide* (ugly, f.s.); /su/ *soul* (drunk, m.s.); /sul/ *soule* (drunk, f.s.); /pla/ *plat* (flat, m.s.); /plat/ *platte* (flat, f.s.), it is much more effective to derive the masculine from the feminine by the uniform procedure of dropping the final consonant than by adding various consonants to the masculine to form the feminine.

[7] Thus, the phrase structure aspect of transformational grammar is essentially a formalization of immediate constituent analysis, as described earlier, into which processual morphophonemics has likewise been incorporated.

## CHAPTER V. PHONOLOGY

[1] For a historical discussion of the methods of transcription associated with the International Phonetic Association, see Robert William Albright, *The International Phonetic Alphabet: Its Background and Development* (Baltimore: Waverly Press, 1958).

[2] The requirement of transitivity is set up on the assumption that, in any theory of this sort, any phonetic segment can belong to only one phoneme.

[3] These are the so-called inherent features. There are also rela-

tional features of stress, duration, and pitch. For an exposition of binary theory, see Roman Jakobson, C. Gunnar M. Fant, and Morris Halle, *Preliminaries to Speech Analysis, Technical Report No. 13,* January 1952 (Cambridge, Mass.: Acoustics Laboratory, M.I.T., 1952).

[4] The most important of these results is that a very important cue for distinguishing the place of articulation of stop consonants is the nature of the transition to the following vowel, or from the preceding vowel.

[5] For this example, see Henry A. Gleason, Jr., *An Introduction to Descriptive Linguistics,* rev. ed. (New York: Holt, Rinehart and Winston, 1961), p. 284.

[6] The asterisk indicates a hypothetical form.

### CHAPTER VI. LINGUISTIC CHANGE

[1] It is a convention of historical linguistics to use the phrase *same language* when one particular form of speech is the historical continuation of another. Obviously, the synchronic test of mutual intelligibility for "same language" is not operationally possible. A "conceptual experiment" might often lead to negative results; for example, if Old English and Modern English were spoken contemporaneously, they would quite surely not be mutually intelligible.

The question of historical continuity is itself not a trivial one. Thus, for purposes of the present exposition, Modern English is taken to be the direct continuation of Anglo-Saxon (Old English); in fact, however, Modern Standard English is based on the Midlands, whereas the literary Anglo-Saxon language was West Saxon, which was spoken in a different area.

[2] Strictly speaking, such "identity" statements do not necessarily assert strict identity. Ordinarily, we cannot infer in such cases more than that the *s* of Anglo-Saxon was highly similar to that of Modern English, since detailed phonetic evidence regarding the earlier period is generally lacking.

[3] Historical linguists regard the "explanation" of individual cases that fall under sporadic processes to be just as legitimate as those that are attributable to general processes, insofar as they are clearly applicable and the particular case is considered to be "closed."

## CHAPTER VII. TYPES OF LANGUAGE CLASSIFICATION

[1] By a process is meant a class of similar but historically independent changes. Thus a change from voiced to corresponding unvoiced consonants in different languages would be instances of the same process.

[2] English *b* is conventionally described as voiced; it is often, in fact, partially or wholly unvoiced.

[3] Edward Sapir, *Language* (New York: Harcourt, Brace, 1921), especially Chap. VI.

[4] Joseph H. Greenberg, "A Quantitative Approach to the Morphological Typology of Language," *International Journal of American Linguistics,* 26 (July 1960), 178–194.

[5] An obstruent is a consonantal sound in which there is closure of the vocal tract sufficient to produce a noise component (e.g., t, s, z). It is opposed to a sonant which has no such closure (e.g., l, n).

## CHAPTER VIII. SYNCHRONIC UNIVERSALS

[1] The sources of these counts are as follows: French, first 1,000 vowels in Stendhal, *Le rouge et le noir* (Paris: Champion, 1933) —Greenberg; Portuguese, 1,000 vowels on pp. 11, 21, and 31 of Celso Furtado, *Formação economica do Brasil,* 4th ed. (Rio de Janeiro: Editôra Fundo de Cultura, 1961)—Greenberg; Ticuna (South America), 500 vowels on p. 331 of Doris G. Anderson, *Conversational Ticuna* (Peru: Yarinacocha Press, 1962)—Greenberg; Mundu (Africa), 500 vowels on p. 179 of P. Charles Vandame, *Le Ngambay-Moundou* (Dakar: Institut Français d'Afrique Noire, 1913)—Greenberg; Chiricahua, first 1,000 vowels on pp. 5, 10, and 15 of Harry Hoijer, *Chiricahua and Mescalero Apache Texts* (Chicago: University of Chicago Press, 1938)—Greenberg; Bengali, from Charles A. Ferguson and Munier Chowdhury, "The Phonemes of Bengali," *Language,* 36 (January–March, 1960), 22–59.

[2] Albert Valdman, "Les Bases statistiques de l'antériorité articulatoire du français," *Le Français moderne,* Paris , Editions D'Artrey, 27 (April 1955), 102–110.

[3] This is not purely a matter of conceptual classification. Such categories as male, ascending generation, and lineality involve the alignment of kinsmen, correlated with differences of behavior

and attitude, membership in kinship groupings, and so on. Hence, there are behavioral correspondences to the absence of a definitional characteristic that would classify father with mother's brother while excluding father's brother.

## CHAPTER IX. DIACHRONIC GENERALIZATION

[1] This distinction is expressed in Windelband's well-known terminology, which opposes nomothetic (scientific) to idiographic (historical) disciplines.

[2] C. A. Ferguson, "Assumptions About Nasals: A Sample Study in Phonological Universals" in Joseph H. Greenberg, ed., *Universals of Language* (Cambridge, Mass.: M.I.T. Press, 1963), pp. 42–47.

[3] French data as described in Chap. VIII, fn. 1; Latin based on a personal count of the first 1,000 vowels in Cicero's *Letters,* Bk. III, Letters 1, 3, 5, 7, and 9.

[4] Briefly stated, the theory of functional yield is that, other things being equal, the tendency of two sounds to merge will be greater, the fewer the number of meaningful pairs in which they are the sole source of contrast. For an exposition of this thesis, see particularly André Martinet, *Économie des changements phonétiques: traité de phonologie diachronique* (Berne: A. Francke, 1955).

[5] There seem, however, to be some American Indian languages in which the contrast of voiced and voiceless vowel has phonemic status—for example, Comanche, Chontal (Mayan), and Santa Ana.

[6] For these data, see Bernard Bloch, "Studies in Colloquial Japanese IV: Phonemics," *Language,* 26 (January–March 1950), 86–125.

[7] I am following Bloch, *op. cit.,* here. However, such final vowels were recorded by earlier investigators and may well occur in the speech of some Japanese at the present time.

## CHAPTER X. HIGHER-LEVEL EXPLANATIONS

[1] Note that even "individual forms," such as *kuşlar* (birds), are themselves classes of occurrences—that is, types, of which the specific instances in actually pronounced Turkish sentences are

tokens. The relation of the *explanans* to the *explanandum* is one of *relative* generality.

2 The generalization under discussion here is in fact statable in the terminology of binary features. In any language, if there are segments with the features of unvoicing and nasality, there are always segments with the features of voicing and nasality. It is not at all clear to me that advocates of binary theory necessarily rule out such statements by confining themselves to the results for specific languages, which eliminate intralanguage redundancies. This section is therefore meant to illustrate how the elimination of certain aspects of individual language description, if adhered to, may prevent crosslinguistic generalization. It is not intended as an attack on binary theory.

3 An example is Henry Gleason's statement: "The use of correct allophones is more important socially than linguistically. Though obviously of concern to linguists, for many practical reasons, the allophones stand on the margin of his field of study and are in some respects external to language." From *An Introduction to Descriptive Linguistics*, rev. ed. (New York: Holt, Rinehart and Winston, 1961), p. 265.

4 For example, Josselson's Russian word count, which gives separate data for conversational as distinct from narrative passages in Russian, shows, in some instances, significantly different frequencies for the two styles in regard to grammatical categories. (Harry H. Josselson, *The Russian word count and frequency analysis of grammatical categories of standard literary Russian* [Detroit: Wayne University Press, 1953]).

5 Modern transformation theory, however, demonstrates that, when language description is in terms of ordered rules, these rules may parallel actual or probable historical changes. Hence, what in the past were processual physical events become abstract "constructs," which serve to explain contemporary physical events. In this way the notion of internal reconstruction (see Wallace L. Chafe, "Internal Reconstruction in Seneca," *Language*, 35 [July–September 1959], 477–495, and the references to the earlier literature there), which was formerly viewed as the drawing of inferences concerning the past of a language from synchronic data (basically morphophonemic alternations), becomes incorporated into the description. There is here, how-

ever, no possible confusion between the higher-level constructs, which are in some correspondence to past changes, and the present physical realizations, which have been generated by the lowest-level rules.

# A List of Symbols

| | |
|---|---|
| $\sim (\sim \phi \sim \psi)$ | Indicates negation |
| $\sim (\tilde{a})$ | Nasalization |
| $\circ (\b{b})$ | Voicelessness |
| $^c (k^c)$ | Aspiration |
| $= (k=)$ | Non-release |
| $\cdot (s\cdot)$ | Sign of length; thus $s\cdot$ is more prolonged than $s$ |
| $. (\phi.\psi)$ | Conjunction |
| $: (t{:}d = k{:}g)$ | Indicates a proportional relation. For example, $t$ is to $d$ as $k$ is to $g$ |
| $\updownarrow$ | Change of linguistic type in either direction |
| $\leftarrow$ | Is implied by |
| $\rightarrow$ | Implies |
| $>$ | Gives rise to, becomes |
| $<$ | Is derived from |
| $\Vert$ | Encloses phonemic transcription |
| [] | Encloses phonetic transcription |
| {} | Encloses morpheme, the smallest meaningful grammatical element |
| * | Indicates a hypothetical form, one whose former existence is conjectured; or a theoretical construct designed to account for an existing form but not occurring itself |

# Index